how to Change the Games Children play

by **G. S. Don Morris**
Montana State University
Bozeman, Montana

Illustrated by
Mark Sullivan

Burgess Publishing Company
Minneapolis, Minnesota

Consulting Editors to the Publisher

Eloise M. Jaeger
University of Minnesota
Minneapolis, Minnesota

LB
1137
.M675

Robert M. Clayton
Colorado State University
Fort Collins, Colorado

Copyright © 1976 by Burgess Publishing Company
Printed in the United States of America
Library of Congress Card Number 75-46208
SBN 0-8087-1382-5

0   9   8   7   6   5   4

To my family—now I know
why authors thank them

Foreword

This book is different. Instead of the usual game-books which contain descriptions of games and generalized statements of philosophy, this book presents the thesis that the very structure of the game must be analyzed in terms of the specific objective sought — "specific outcome behaviors".

This is an interesting and an important notion. It asks teachers to look at games *before* they use them in their programs, rather than attaching *values* to the games as justification for use; values that may not be there due to the very structure of the game.

The second notion of the book, and equally important for educational use of games, is the plea for alternatives and changes in the structure of games. This, Dr. Morris suggests, will include more students. The exclusion of students who *need* to participate will be diminished and perhaps will even disappear.

Dr. Morris offers a model for the analysis of games and guidelines for discovering and creating new ones. These operational tools can serve an excellent means for the teacher who has to interpret models into practical ways of "doing it."

Throughout the book the author projects a sense of respect for the individual's ability to think, to feel, to make decisions and to cooperate with others — to join together in both the analysis and design of games and the sheer enjoyment of playing them.

Muska Mosston

Preface

This book is designed for everyone who teaches games to youngsters—elementary, secondary teachers, physical educators, special educators and recreation leaders. Games have become an integral part of our society as leisure activities as well as within an educational setting. Individuals play games and yet the games people play prevent a high percentage of the participants from experiencing successful outcomes. This book attempts to demonstrate how someone can structure a game to account for individual differences as well as promote specific behavioral outcomes.

Having read the book and understood the concepts, it is entirely possible that you will not have to purchase another games book. There is more than one way to play a game.

I wish to thank my elementary students in Eugene, Oregon and Bozeman, Montana for demonstrating to me that the games analysis concept really does work. In addition I would like to express thanks to my high school students in Upland, California for prompting me to reconsider what games are really all about. Special thanks are extended to Carol Sanford and Miriam Hoereth for typing, organizing and evaluating the pages of this book and to Mark Sullivan for his interesting drawings. Finally, I realize now why writers thank their families—Thanks!

G.S. "Don" Morris

Contents

Foreward v

Preface vii

1 **Roles Games Play** 1

2 **Games Analysis Explained** 11

Games Analysis Model **12**
Games Analysis Grid **16**

3 **The Many Uses of Games Analysis** 18

Student Decision Making Via Games Analysis **18**
Decision Making and Social-Emotional Response **23**
New Games from Old **25**
Lead-up Games Developing Specific Motor Skills **27**
Problem Solving Via Games Analysis **36**

4 **Methods of Presenting Games Analysis to Elementary and Secondary Youngsters** 44

Secondary **44**
Elementary **45**
Exceptional Children **47**

5 Observation and Assessment Alternatives 50

Assessment Tool **53**

6 Examples of Games Designed for Specific Movement Areas 71

Softball Type Games **71**
  Elementary **72**
  Secondary **82**
Volleyball Type Games **83**
  Elementary **84**
  Secondary **91**
Basketball Type Games **94**
  Elementary **95**
  Secondary **105**
Tag and Relay Games **111**
  Tag **112**
  Relay **113**

7 Some Closing Thoughts 122

Appendix—Factors and Choices 125

Chapter

1

Roles
Games Play

We are in the age of credibility, objectivity and accountability in all facets of education. Never in the modern era of teaching have we been involved in so much inspection and introspection regarding what we teach and how we teach it. One can pick up almost any educational journal and read an article on educational accountability accomplished through competency based teaching.

Within the field of physical education a great deal has recently been accomplished establishing movement competencies for specific skills, e.g., dribbling a ball 10 feet, performing two forward rolls in a tucked position. A major emphasis in our field seems to be inspection of selected areas within the movement world in terms of evaluation measurement possibilities, rather than understanding the relationships between existing movement activity structures and resultant participant behavior (physical, emotional, social, intellectual). The movement experiences collectively identified as games in a physical education curriculum have undergone little inspection relative to desired specific educational outcomes. For that matter, the games curriculum has not really changed at all over the last fifty years. A critical analysis of what games really do for and to youngsters has not really been done. Yet it is quite apparent that youngsters up to at least age 11 or 12 love to engage in game activities. The activity and excitement generated by games produce enthusiasm on the part of most youngsters. The youngsters enjoy demonstrating their skill and games certainly allow them to perform before a captive audience, specifically their peers.

A multitude of rationales are offered for having games as a part of the physical education program in elementary schools. The following are examples of the most quoted reasons for including games in a school setting:

1. Games promote physical growth and development.
2. Games promote the socialization process.
3. Games aid in development of motor skills.
4. Games help develop emotional understanding between and within youngsters.
5. Games can use up excess energy on the part of youngsters.
6. Games need to be learned for use as adults during leisure time moments.

Not one of these game purposes will be served in a game unless the game is structured to promote the specific behavior. Thus it is important to understand that the structure and design of every game played mandate, dictate, elicit very specific resultant behaviors, and if certain outcomes are desired from a game then the game must be structured accordingly.

We often hear that games promote physical growth and development. This is true up to a point. A growing youngster needs physical activity to stimulate growth and development of the body. However, certain games can and do cause harm simply because their structure predisposes the youngsters to injury. If a youngster plays a standardized game (rules, equipment type are all predetermined), then individual differences are not accounted for. T-ball baseball for youngsters aged eight and under is an example of a standardized game. All the youngsters use balls of the same size, color, and weight. Research has shown that the three preceding descriptive variables of the ball, along with several other variables, influence the ability of elementary school youngsters to see, track, perceive, and finally react to the ball. Youngsters' eyes and their visual perceptual process seem to undergo a series of developmental steps which are not necessarily age-related. In other words, some youngsters at age eight will strike, field, and catch the white ball well simply because they have a more mature visual perceptual process. Those youngsters who possess less mature visual perceptual processes will not catch the fly ball, will not stop a grounder coming toward them with the possible result of a ball hitting the teeth, eyes, or other vital parts and causing injury. Another example of game structure often not promoting growth and development of the body is too much stress placed on a youngster's elbow when pitching too long. Over a period of time the growth plate area in the elbow region can be affected by too much physical stress. The National Organization of Little League has recognized that stress on the elbow can retard growth; thus they changed the structure of the game so that a youngster can only pitch six innings per week. It is now accepted that growth and development of the body can be affected by stress, including stress promoted by game structure and/or design.

Games are said to promote the socialization processes in elementary youngsters. This concept presupposes that one knows what the socialization process is. The concept of socialization is very complex and broad, therefore it is difficult to define. Basically one can make the following statements about the socialization process:

1. As human beings we learn to be social beings.
2. Individuals must learn to participate effectively and efficiently in social groups.
3. Elkin (1960) suggests that socialization as a process allows a human being to comprehend the ways of a society so that he or she can operate effectively within it.
4. Interaction occurs between the society and/or social group and the individual learns how to manage this interaction stage.
5. Socialization is a continuous process that occurs throughout one's lifetime.
6. Roles of an individual within a social group are defined for each of us.

In addition to understanding the process of socialization it is also important to understand that there are a variety of modalities through which an individual becomes socialized. Physical education is but one of the many means used to foster socialization skills and within this curriculum we suggest that games and specifically competitive games help promote the socialization process. As physical educators we have professed the value of game participation in determining social roles and identities and developing social skills but we have made very few attempts to ascertain whether or not participation in games validates this point of view. Do games really teach youngsters to cooperate? Do games promote valuable social interaction among players when, by design, two opposing football teams meet on the field and immediately upon completion of the game head for the locker room without even talking to one another? Is this promotion of social interaction? Does participation in relay games help foster cooperative behavior among relay participants and between relay teams when the sole behavior, by design, is to perform a motor behavior and tag the next teammate then sit quietly at the end of the team? How much and what kind of interaction is really being displayed? Often what we as teachers think happens is not even close to what actually occurs in a game simply because the structure and design of a game does not allow it to occur.

Look in many elementary physical education texts and you will see that in a typical lesson plan that uses the medium of games, the author will suggest concluding the day's lesson with a game utilizing the individual skills. This idea is suggested because the games are thought to enhance the development of motor skills. How many times have each of us experienced the following? After individually practicing the hand dribble with each youngster demonstrating some degree of movement efficiency, we next play a dribbling relay, only to discover how inefficiently the youngsters are now controlling the ball, losing it, dribbling it too far away from their bodies, and so on. To practice one specific movement model, e.g., chest pass, and then expect youngsters to incorporate the skill efficiently into a dynamic and changing game is of little benefit to them simply because most game outcomes and/or situations are unpredictable. Riley (1975) suggests the following: "Learning experiences must be based on an analysis of the total movement demands of various games. Consequently, a more comprehensive definition of skill and a different approach to teaching game skills is warranted." Barrett (1973) also suggests that an efficient mover possesses "versatility and dexterity in his ability to move . . . in movement situations that are both planned and unexpected." Again, by structuring a game in a particular way, the performance of the motor skills is greatly affected, usually to the detriment of the performance. A simple example of this concept is demonstrated when youngsters are asked to pass the ball back and forth to each other so that each performer controls the ball and does not drop it. The teacher then introduces a game that requires the participants to see which couple can pass the ball between themselves 20 times—first couple reaching 20 is the winner. One wonders whether the game is designed to promote efficient motor control of the ball or to see which couple is the fastest. What do you think happens most often in this situation? Experience shows that in most cases youngsters try to finish regardless of the type of motor behavior exhibited. The efficient mechanical principles demonstrated earlier in the lesson simply disappear in this game because *by design* the game indicates to the youngsters that it is important to reach 20 passes first even though you tell them to "pass the ball correctly with good form." In a close race with another couple it is most interesting to watch the "new way" to pass the ball to a teammate. Another claim for games is that through proper lead up games one can progressively develop motor skills from easy to more difficult. This certainly presupposes that teachers analyze each game relative to the factors that influence the game and thus dictate performance for each class of youngsters and for each youngster in their class. The concept of task analysis will be expanded upon in a later chapter. Suffice it to say that anyone who does not first understand the factors that comprise a motor skill will not be able to design a movement activity (game) that accounts for each individual youngster's present ability. Games must consider a youngster's present growth and development stage as this stage influences the youngster's ability to perform motor tasks efficiently and thus exhibit some degree of skill within the game.

Another unique quality that games seem to possess is their ability to help develop emotional understanding between and within youngsters. Unless this specific behavior is accounted for within the structure of a game then simply wishing for it to occur is like waiting for the pot of gold at the end of the rainbow. How many times have you witnessed a games situation where one player will become very aware of another teammate's inability to perform and say, "Charlie, you blockhead, can't you catch anything except a cold?" Most of us have overheard such inter-jections as "Oh, boy, we've got old butterfingers Billie on our team—how about it, butterfingers, think you can catch *one* ball today?" or "Just 'cuz you dropped the ball we lost, you do that again and I'll knock your block off!" Certainly this last remark would make each one of us feel emotionally secure within the context of a game situation! The point is that youngsters are often placed in emotional settings that they cannot deal with effectively, such settings being the direct result of the game structure that mandates an emotional outburst on the part of players if success and/or failure results. Some games seem to make the youngsters more aware of their own mistakes and those of their teammates. Many games also produce excitable behavior that does not contri-bute positively to the game outcome. As a result some youngsters say, "I quit cuz I'm not allowed to bat, they pinch hit for me all the time." How many times have you seen an elementary youngster feign an injury upon failure to execute a major skill? What is the youngster saying to you, to me, to us who are educators? Youngsters need to understand their limitations, and for this reason this book does not advocate a "positive experience" for every youngster every moment of his life. As educators we do, however, need to be aware that continuously placing youngsters into emotional predicaments they cannot handle is detrimental to adequate emotional development. Games that are structured to produce one winner all the time with concomitant social evaluation of winner and loser cause statements and concerns like some of the previously mentioned verbal exchanges. By structuring a game in a particular fashion, a teacher can take the basic interest off "beating the other team" and allow each team to concentrate on its own performance. Understanding of this concept is vital if we expect games to be used as a viable development medium in physical education.

Another selling point for games is that the games help "burn off" the extra energy all elementary youngsters demonstrate from time to time. A first reaction to this statement is that the youngsters may be telling us something about their previous time spent in the classroom—could it be that the "excess" energy is simply a manifestation of boredom? Research also suggests that "burning off" the excess energy produces only a temporary change in youngsters' movement behavior due to their amazing recuperative powers. Within a short period of time they are "antsy" again if the same situation that precipitated the behavior still exists. If, on the other hand, the youngsters are moved to exhaustion one needs to ask if they will continue to enjoy movement activity if a negative value is consistently attached to the motor activity. Perhaps one should provide them with a strategy to employ when they start to get "hyper," such as neuromuscular relaxation. Perhaps one needs to ascertain why the youngsters need to move and make the appropriate adjustments. Finally, just as it is our job to teach the youngsters how to move efficiently upon energy activation, it should also be our role to teach them how to move efficiently upon energy deactivation, i.e., slowdown. Knowing how to slow down is a learned behavior, and it should be part of an elementary curriculum.

Games must be played so we can learn the rules, thus allowing us some activity to perform during our leisure time as adults. How many middle-aged and older folks have you seen playing 5 x 5 basketball as a regular diet? Admittedly some of us do play this particular sport, but to sell the idea of including games in the elementary curriculum in order to develop leisure time sports is not defensible. When was the last time your major form of physical activity consisted of a tag game, relay game and NCAA basketball game? This is not to suggest that certain leisure time games can't be learned but it should not serve as the rationale for including games in a physical education curriculum.

Thus there exists a need for alternatives in utilizing games in our elementary physical education curriculum. We need to evaluate the role games are to play in providing educational outcomes for youngsters. As Mauldon and Redfern (1969) suggest: "The point at issue, however, is not so much which games should be taught but whether, and in what ways, the essential features of playing a game afford opportunities for an extension of experience which is profitable for all." Many elementary teachers (80% of elementary P.E. around the U.S. is taught by the classroom teacher) do not regard games as a highly relative part of their curriculum. Often the games are used to give the teachers a few minutes of rest during the day. Analyzing most report cards found in elementary schools, very little is mentioned regarding the youngster's development stage in games. Usually one finds the following assessment criteria applied to elementary physical education: 1. Your youngster is developing body skills; 2. Your youngster is developing game skills. One also discovers a check mark in one of three assessment descriptors: Commendable, Acceptable and/or Needs improvement. Does this typical report card identify the contributing factors or components that elicit specific behaviors? Do the assessment descriptors suggest to either the parent, child or teacher what the youngster is currently capable of doing, should be doing, ought to be doing in terms of specific behaviors? Don't parents, teachers, and children need information describing the development of behavior within a game's context? Finally, does this report card suggest that perhaps, just perhaps, we don't fully understand what games are, can do for, and can do against the children that participate?

The structure of a game, i.e., the design, dramatically influences the behavioral outcomes displayed by the participants. Let us consider a few examples of this concept.

A. The structure of a running file relay predisposes various teams to become most concerned with the order of finish. This relay allows four or more teams to be in file order next to each other as shown on the next page.

X X X X
X X X X
X X X X
X X X X

The object of the relay is to run, one at a time, over to and around a traffic cone, return to the team, and tag the the next runner, who repeats the task. The race is over when everyone has completed the task. The team completing the task first is declared the winner.

Simply because the teams are positioned next to each other, each member of each team has a clear view of the status of the race. This is both good and bad. Experience has shown that the youngsters spend more time worrying about the finish of the race than upon their own performance (relative to movement efficiency). Certain social behaviors result: (1) extreme pleasure exhibited by the winners; (2) anguish exhibited by the losers, the intensity of which increases if you are last; (3) certain verbal admonishments among and between teams.

This is not meant to suggest that this is occurring all the time everywhere in the U.S., but by design game attention, concern, and performance assessment become the primary focus. Is this what a teacher wants? If yes, why? If no, what are the alternatives?

B. The height of a basketball rim from the ground in most schools is held constant although adjustable basketball backboards are now available. The standard height tends to affect the motor ability of basketball shooting, particularly for the less skilled. The game design that suggests the basket remain at one constant height therefore affects the motor ability of youngsters. Several suggestions relative to a solution are found in chapter 6.

C. At a local elementary school a favorite game of the youngsters is "One Behind." The teacher performs a physical move or maintains a particular physical posture. The youngsters must copy the physical move or posture, but only after the teacher has performed the next move. Thus, the youngsters are memorizing the next movement position but they stay one move behind the teacher. This game is very similar to Simon Says, but no youngster is eliminated from the game as in Simon Says. The teacher controls the tempo of the game and if a child makes a

FILE RELAY PATTERN

mistake he can either look at his peers for help or the teacher begins a new game. This game is excellent for developing visual short term memory. The important concept here is that by design all youngsters are included, not excluded, and also all youngsters perform the motor tasks efficiently.

The previous three examples illustrate that the way a game is designed affects the resultant student behavior in most instances. To insist that elementary youngsters below age 10 involve themselves in only the "national" games for physical education class is placing too great a degree of difficulty upon their shoulders in terms of performing the behaviors required within the restrictive guidelines of the games. The time has come to critically evaluate the role of games in our educational world. It is necessary to understand the influence game design has upon mandating specific social, emotional, physical, and intellectual outcomes. Riley (1975) describes this new direction well when she states: "Learning to participate effectively and purposefully in games should be a vital part of every child's education. To implement this belief so that the experience is personally meaningful requires a different approach to the teaching of games."

The next chapter introduces a tool that both teachers and youngsters can use to aid better structure within a game in order to enhance specific resultant behaviors. This tool is called GAMES ANALYSIS.

References

Barrett, Kate. "I wish I Could Fly" in *Contemporary Philosophies of Physical Education and Athletics,* edited by Robert Cobb and Paul Lepley. Columbus, Ohio: Charles E. Merrill Publishing Co., 1973.

Elkin, F. *The Child and Society.* New York: Random House, 1960.

Mauldon, E., and Redfern, H. B. *Games Teaching.* London: MacDonald and Evans, 1969.

Riley, Marie. "Games and Humanism." *JOHPER,* February 1975, pp. 46-49.

Chapter

2

Games Analysis Explained

What is games analysis? Essentially it is an attempt to provide a framework or model from which any movement game can be analyzed and investigated in the sense that game structure mandates specific outcome behaviors. Games analysis attempts to answer the question, "What is the same among all movement games?" Many items consistently found in games have either a simple or a complex structure. All of our movement games include players, rules, equipment, social behaviors of competition and cooperation, organizational patterns, and rationales for playing the game. There are undoubtedly some more items that help comprise a game. Pause for a moment and try to think of some additional items consistently found in movement games.

Now that you have had time to think of these game items, analyze them and begin to categorize them into groups that seem to "fit together." By categorizing the items you are organizing your thoughts, making the concept of game parts more manageable. At the same time you are beginning to establish a model which can be used to design games to meet a wide variety of behavioral objectives.

Several authors in elementary physical education have suggested a variety of categories within a movement game structure. Kirchner (1974) offers to use the following game categories: number of players, playing space, rules, and equipment. Mosston (1966) suggests categories such as: number of participants, organizational patterns, equipment movement, purpose, and limits.

Mauldon and Redfern (1970) suggest the following game categories: apparatus, playing areas, rules and number per side.

Regardless of the labels attached to the game categories there are six categories which have been used successfully over the past seven years. Within each of the six categories there exists a wide choice of components as demonstrated in the table on the opposite page. Examples of components are items listed under each category heading.

By categorizing the many components that make up a game, one is able to provide a model from which teachers and students are able to design, change, adapt and make decisions about the entire structure of any game previously played or any game needed to be played to enhance specific motoric, social and emotional outcomes.

GAMES ANALYSIS MODEL

For years I have designed and adapted games using the categories opposite as a basis for my game model. This is how the model works.

A game is divided into six categories with each category consisting of a number of components. Thus a concrete description of the game can be demonstrated to most anyone. Table 2-1 attempts to illustrate a variety of components taken randomly from quite a few games and sports—the list of components is certainly far from complete. The game components thereby become additional descriptors of a specific game. The games analysis model allows the individual teacher to study any game he or she teaches, participates in, or watches and dissect that game's components into the six categories. Once this step is completed, it is possible to provide a wide range of educational experiences by changing the components of one or more categories dependent upon what the teacher wants to occur on the field or in the gym. To manipulate components and/or categories constructively involves both the teacher and students in a *games analysis process.* Through careful, considerate, intelligent, analytical adjustment of a game design specific social, emotional, intellectual, and physical behaviors can be planned for within the game experience.

TABLE 2-1.
GAMES ANALYSIS MODEL-CATEGORIES AND COMPONENTS

Players	Equipment	Movement Pattern	Organizational Pattern	Limitations	Purpose
individual	balls	running	random placement	3 outs/inning	to win
2/team	bats	jumping	circle	10 yds for 1st down	to promote cooperative behavior
3/team	sticks	hopping	columns	boundaries on field	help develop locomotor skills
4/team	gloves	skipping	double circles	5 min./quarter	promotes problem-solving behavior
5/team	hoops	walking	files	tag below waist	aids in eye-hand coordination
six on one team, four on another	plastic bottles	galloping	double columns	only 5 players per team	helps develop self concept
even number on one team, odd number on other	ropes	kicking	staggered file	4 downs to make a T.D.	develop competitive spirit
	bases	throwing	even/odd file	must dribble the ball for every step taken	promotes sportsmanship
	wands	catching	diamond		
???	bowling pins	twisting	triangle	???	develop cardio-vascular fitness
	individual body parts	rolling	square		
	???	???	???		

T-BALL BASEBALL

TABLE 2-2.
GAMES ANALYSIS GRID

Name of Game	Players	Equipment	Movement Pattern	Purpose	Organizational Pattern	Limitations	Description
1. Basketball	5/team	1 basketball	running, jumping shooting	score most points	zone	NCAA rules	A brief game description would follow
2. Basketball	5/team	1 basketball	running, jumping shooting	score most points	man-man	NCAA rules	A brief game description would follow

GAMES ANALYSIS GRID

To aid the teachers and students, a games analysis grid has been devised to aid in the analysis of games and sports. The grid simply lists the six categories of a game and provides a space for the game title and game descriptors. The teacher or the students can place the given game's component descriptors into the appropriate categories. A typical grid, definitely incomplete, for two games of basketball is shown in Table 2-2, illustrating the manipulation of one game category:

The grid shown demonstrates how the game of basketball can be described by placing its components within the appropriate categories. The grid becomes a formula for the game of basketball, i.e., using the stated components within the categories one begins to play the game.

Initially you will find it necessary to include in the grid a section that verbally describes how one would play the game. After a period of time it may no longer be necessary to include this section as you will find it quite easy to describe the game by simply reading across the grid categories. It is important to understand that the description section is not a necessary category that affects the use of the games analysis concept—it is simply an aid to folks who are just beginning to use the games analysis model. The example used also demonstrates a specific use of the grid—keep all categories constant, change one or more components in one category, and you have another basketball *type* game. More regarding this procedure will be found in the next chapter.

Changing, adapting, or designing a game should be accomplished while keeping specific educational outcomes in mind. If you want specific motor activities to be enhanced the games must be designed to account for the current growth and development status of the performers; in addition you must have the knowledge to examine other factors that may influence the youngsters' ability to perform the task. An example of this is found within the game of T-ball baseball.

In T-ball baseball, the baseball is placed upon a stationary batting tee and the batter strikes the ball off of the tee. T-ball is played with youngsters eight years and younger. Now, this game takes into consideration the youngster's current stage of growth and development; at the same time it identifies a factor that influences performance of the striking motor behavior. The eight-and-under youngster's visual-perceptual apparatus is far from mature in terms of tracking a moving object. Research indicates that youngsters of this age can more efficiently track horizontally and vertically moving balls than balls that travel in a large arc. Thus T-ball, by design, allows for this behavior to a degree by utilizing a batting tee. In addition the game has identified two factors that influence whether or not the youngsters can successfully strike the ball. We call them the method of trajectory factor and the angle of trajectory factor. We know that youngsters eight years old and under can hit a stationary ball in the horizontal plane more efficiently than a ball which is moving in a variety of planes. This last concept is known as task analysis. Certainly elimination of the pitcher may "save" young players' arms as well as speed up the offensive part of the game.

Over the next few chapters information will be given regarding task analysis and other pertinent concepts with which one should be familiar in order to change, adapt, or design a game. First, it is important to know how to change a game via games analysis; second, you must have information that allows you to make appropriate changes in order to elicit proper educational outcomes. Just as there are developmental stages in the physical channel of education, so there appear also to be developmental stages within the intellectual, emotional, and social channels. The manipulation of the components in the games analysis categories can be accomplished in a manner which will provide many educational experiences for the student as well as aid the teacher in designing or adapting existing games in the school curriculum.

References

Kirchner, Glenn. *Physical Education for Elementary School Children.* Dubuque, Iowa: William C. Brown Co., 1974.

Mauldon, E., and Redfern, H. B. *Games Teaching.* London: MacDonald and Evans, 1970, p. 77.

Mosston, Muska. *Teaching Physical Education.* Columbus, Ohio: Charles E. Merrill Co., 1966.

Chapter

The Many Uses of Games Analysis

Games analysis is a process through which specific educational behaviors result. According to Webster, a process is a "series of actions or operations definitely conducing to an end" and a process is also "any phenomenon which shows a continuous change in time, as the process of growth." Therefore, when utilizing the games analysis concept, you must not only identify the factors that influence performance but you must also consider the behavioral outcomes that you want obtained from each game. Now this may sound like you are taking the fun out of games. It is not intended that way. If games are to be considered part of an educational experience, let us simply plan for those experiences by designing the games so that they can be realized.

It will take time to understand the process of games analysis. By adjusting game structures in an orderly manner it is possible to enhance the total development of a youngster. Teachers and students alike need to undergo a change of attitude regarding the structure and uses of games. This chapter will attempt to show you some of the uses games can be put to in terms of enriching the education of our youth.

STUDENT DECISION MAKING VIA GAMES ANALYSIS

If decision making is a necessary skill for youngsters to possess and if decision making is a learned process then it logically seems to follow that an opportunity needs to be given to the child to make decisions. An opportunity to make decisions is given when the teacher allows the youngsters to change the structure of a game to meet the motoric, emotional, and social needs of an individual youngster or a group of youngsters. This is accomplished by allowing the youngsters to change or manipulate one or more of the components within a given category or categories. The youngsters feel that they have some control over their environment. This change in and of itself is often enough to allow many youngsters a feeling of security within the "game world." Moreover, the feeling of security often dramatically enhances performance. Mosston (1966) has written a great deal about the decision-making process within the educational world: "Now, neither teacher nor student can make decisions in a vacuum. Decisions are always made about something. This 'something' is the subject matter of teaching and learning." Mosston certainly saw the teaching-learning act as a shift in decision-making responsibility. Depending on the amount, types, and who made the decisions, certain types of behavior would result. If all of the decisions all of the time were made by the teacher a certain kind of learning would occur. If decision-making responsibility was shifted to the student via an individualization *process* then another kind of learning would occur and a certain type of individual would emerge. Mosston suggests that the shift in decision making to the student produces "the free man whom a free society wishes to produce through its education—education for a society of independent people. Independence implies the ability to make choices among convictions; it connotes the strength to act and pursue the chosen convictions."

The following hierarchy, developed over the past seven years, lists the categories within the games analysis model in which elementary and secondary students seem to be able to accept immediate decision-making responsibility.

> Initially the teacher controls the game environment by making all of the decisions about the game for all of the youngsters. When game structure decisions are gradually relinquished to the youngsters in a prescribed manner the youngsters learn how complex game design is, how one game category relates to another, and how to deal with the responsibility that accompanies any decision-making process.
> At all grade levels, 3-12, it is suggested that the students first be allowed to alter the type of movement employed

during the game. Next allow them to change the number of players per team; follow this by allowing them to alter, adjust, or change the equipment or change the type of equipment being used.

With changes in more than one category it will be found that the limitation category must be adjusted as well. Experience over the past three years has shown that while you can change one component in one category without having to change the limitation category, as soon as you change one component in two or more categories you usually have to change or add another component to the limitation category. The following example illustrates this concept:

Let us assume that a group of sixth graders are playing a game of traditional 5 X 5 basketball employing NCAA basketball rules. It is possible to let the youngsters change a specific movement pattern without having to adjust any of the rules. Let's say they allow only underhand shooting—it is not necessary to adjust any of the stated NCAA rules unless it is felt necessary to sanction non-underhanded shooting.

Now let us say the youngsters change yet another movement component which allows the players to run with the ball. If in addition to this change the youngsters allow seven players/team to be on the court at the same time (player category) and they also add another ball to the game (equipment category), then indeed you must change the limitation category.

It is important that the teacher initially be the person to decide which category will be altered; then as the youngsters learn how to function within this decision-making environment they can begin to make their own decisions regarding game structure. The specific techniques for promoting games analysis within the elementary and secondary school are presented in chapter 4.

The following story illustrates the effect relinquishing certain decisions to students has upon game design:

Several years ago I introduced the games analysis concept to a heterogenous group of ninth grade physical education students. It was quite a learning experience for the students as well as for me. After several weeks using the games analysis concept, the students developed one of the most interesting and exciting games that I have ever seen. To begin with, the game was meant to be a softball *type* of game. Part of their assignment was to develop a game that would account for all of the motoric needs of *each* student in the class (38 students). They chose to allow each player to decide what piece of equipment to use when at bat. For example, the highest skilled student chose to use a regulation softball bat and a regulation softball thrown to the batter in the traditional manner. On the other hand, the least skilled student chose to have a large rubber ball rolled toward him and he had to strike the rolling ball with an oversized, underweighted bat. There were many other equipment modifications, but these two examples describe the decision-making extremes. With the equipment changes the students soon learned that there needed to be specific rule changes accompanying the equipment modifications. The resultant game was enthusiastically played by *all* the students because the game structure did not automatically exclude youngsters due to their motor ability. As a matter of fact, the youngsters soon made other changes in their game as they became necessary, and they also seemed to gain a more cooperative spirit within the group. These students revelled in the spirit of decision making relative to physical education class. Slowly but surely they began to understand that individuals were different and that it was all right to possess the physical skills each had at the time.

We often say that we should teach individuals, but rarely in a college methods course do we receive information on how to accomplish this within a game framework. Teaching younsters how to make appropriate, responsible decisions can go a long way in terms of promoting the individual respect one person has for another. It is of utmost importance that we as teachers realize that decision making is a *learned* process—a process that does not occur for all groups or individuals at the same rate.

Identify those decisions that youngsters can handle and build upon them. It is likewise important to teach the students strategies to employ when and if the decision they made was inappropriate. For example, if a group of your students changed the equipment category in the game of baseball so that a golf ball was used as the ball, you need to provide this group of students with a strategy.

EXAMPLES OF SOFTBALL-TYPE GAME

Within the scope of this situation, it may be appropriate to ask the group first of all to consider the safety of using such a ball in light of the poor visibility the ball would exhibit—someone could get hurt if they couldn't track the ball. Thus you have provided this group of youngsters with an analysis strategy—they must analyze the effect the equipment change may have on the catching performance of the youngsters playing the game. You the teacher can now control the decisions that are made within a game. The grid on the next page (Table 3-1) demonstrates a procedure for relinquishing decisions.

Allowing students to make decisions within a game needs to be done with a purpose in mind. The types and amounts of decisions that you allow the students to make should allow for some kind of education experience to be engaged in.

DECISION MAKING AND SOCIAL-EMOTIONAL RESPONSE

How many times have you introduced a game that you are quite excited with, usually something you learned at a recent workshop, convention, or school visitation, only to have your students act as if the plague had struck? What went wrong? Was the game too difficult, too easy? Should you dismiss the game permanently? No!! Perhaps it was only a part of the game that caused the students to react as they did. Perhaps if only one category in the game were changed the students would enjoy playing the game. The structure of the game often dictates the resultant student behavior. If the students are misbehaving while playing the game and it isn't just one of those days, ask yourself why rather than react emotionally. It may be that the movement tasks dictated by the present game structure are preventing certain students from any possible success. Youngsters of all ages compensate for movement inability with inappropriate social behavior. Given the opportunity to have some degree of success, most youngsters will not display inappropriate behavior. Allow *them* to make some of the decisions regarding the structure of the game to be played. There is a reason for every behavior displayed by a youngster; whether it is a physiological or an environmental reason is not the issue. As teachers we can, to a degree, begin to control environmental factors that precipitate inappropriate social and emotional behaviors. First identify the youngster who is having difficulty, then try to identify the factor or factors causing the problem. This

TABLE 3-1.
RELINQUISHING DECISIONS VIA GAMES ANALYSIS GRID

Name of Game	Players	Equipment	Movement Pattern	Organizational Pattern	Limitations	Purpose
1. Volleyball	6/side	1 volleyball	Striking, running, spiking, setting	2 rows of three	NCAA rules	to win
2. Same	same	same	Striking, open hand,* spiking, setting	same	same	same
3. Same	same	2 plastic balls		same	adjust rules	same
4. Same	7/team	3 plastic balls		1 row of three 1 row of four	adjust rules	allow more to play

*Underline signifies change from previous game.

is a difficult task for each of us to master; it takes a great deal of time, insight, and practice. What you will find happening is that often the inappropriate behavior of "clowning around," not paying attention, or "making fun" of someone else's performance is the result of an inability to perform adequately within the game. You can begin to solve this problem by changing the game or asking the youngster to change the game. Both strategies have been employed with students from third grade through twelfth grade with a high degree of success (measured by improved emotional control and socially appropriate behavior). Strangely enough, this strategy also allows you, the teacher, some emotional comfort. It is quite trying to experience a situation in which the students are at each other's throats, particularly if you had a rough night previous to the day's lessons. You can now take solace in applying the analysis concept which should promote student behavioral change, which in turn will make your day a bit brighter or more bearable.

NEW GAMES FROM OLD

It has been suggested previously that teachers and students alike can design new games from existing traditional games. There are many reasons why one would want to do just this. You may want to design another game that approximates the traditional game so that the youngsters can develop certain skills. For example, you want to introduce your class to the traditional game of volleyball because you are interested in the game and because you believe that the game will help develop good hand-eye coordination. You work for a few days on some of the basic skills and feel that the youngsters are now ready for a game. Unfortunately, after five minutes of play the students become bored and start to hit the ball everywhere except where it should be going. Some of the students seemingly could care less if the ball came within a foot of them; they are becoming very restless. What should you do? Again, the first thing is to analyze your game. Can each student perform the basic skills involved? If the answer is no, what factors are the cause? Could the equipment being used possibly be a limiting factor? Instead of using a traditional leather ball try a plastic ball (often found at large displays in grocery stores). Often just the change in the equipment being used is enough to promote game success, particularly with younger students.

Let's continue with our volleyball game for a moment more. Suppose you have introduced the game to a group of fifth and

sixth grade youngsters—this is the first time they have played the game. You also want to teach them the traditional game of volleyball, but after three minutes you realize that the game is not going just as you planned. The students are missing the ball, they are consistently hitting the ball into the net as well as hitting the ball four or five times on one side. What should you do?

Again, look at the game in terms of the skills necessary to play the game. Are the students able to perform the skills? Let's assume in this instance that they can each individually perform the skills but when they are asked to perform in this group setting something happens. What, if anything, seems to affect their ability to get the ball over the net? Could it be the equipment? If yes, change the ball or adjust the net height off the ground. Teachers often set the net at arm's length height, only to produce frustration on the part of the students. Now let's assume that the youngsters can begin to get the ball over the net with some degree of regularity but many are still having difficulty returning the ball after they hit it once. It is suggested that you, the teacher, mandate a rule change. Allow the youngsters to hit the ball three, four, or five times if they need to gain control over the ball before returning the ball to the net. If our goal is to get youngsters interested in a game let's not deprive them of the enjoyment of succeeding before they develop all of the necessary motor skills. It just may be that many youngsters need the extra time of the "additional" hits to gain control over the ball before returning the ball to the other side. We in physical education should strive for motoric control of our body parts rather than seek quantity results (how far, how fast). By allowing a slight rule change in the traditional game of volleyball you have provided the students with new hopes for success.

If you don't want to call these "new" games by their traditional name, make up your own names. If a game does not promote the reaction that you expected, take a moment to analyze why. The beginning teacher utilizing the games analysis concept may want to write out the traditional game in a grid. Then by inspection of several of the categories you can begin to find solutions for replaying the game. You have now developed "new" games from the "old" games. See the chapters for each specific sport for additional game designs.

LEAD-UP GAMES DEVELOPING
SPECIFIC MOTOR SKILLS

As physical educators we are aware of the fact that we should provide games that lead into the traditional or terminal game. We call these games lead-ups. If we are going to teach the students the game of football we should not expect them to be able to play the game of football efficiently on the very first day. Rather we develop over a period of days and/or weeks the skills necessary to play the game. Thus we play lead-up games that require the use of these developing skills. In this way we gradually introduce the students to the skills and concepts of football. Game analysis can help the teacher program the development of the motor skills and game concepts necessary for participation in the game. How? Each teacher has individual preferences in teaching sports skills. It is not the purpose here to suggest what these skill progressions should or should not be. Rather the intention is to demonstrate how a teacher can use the games analysis concept via utilization of the grid to help plan, over a period of time, specific lead-up games terminating in the final game objective.

First decide on the terminal game objective in terms of skill requirement and concept involvement. Basically you are writing behavioral objectives for the day's lesson. Write this game in the grid. Next plan how and when you will teach specific motor skills and game concepts. Let's assume that a typical teaching session allows for warm-up activities, followed by introduction and practice of the skills to be learned that day. Finally you may decide to end the day's session with some kind of game activity (relay or lead-up game). Of course, this regimen will not be followed each day, as no two teachers follow exactly the same pattern of skill teaching. Let's see now how one can develop some lead-up games. The example used will be football at the sixth grade level. Notice the stated behavioral objectives relative to psycho-motor development (motor) and congitive development (concepts). Each objective can be observed and measured.

UNIT—Football Skills and Concepts
OBJECTIVES—Motor:
Develop ability to pass the football a distance of 10 yards with accuracy; hand the ball off without fumbling the ball; center the ball with accuracy a distance of 5 feet; punt the football with accuracy a distance of 15 yards; catch a thrown football 10 feet, five of 10 attempts, display ability to run with the ball; demonstrate ability to screen block.
OBJECTIVES—Concepts:
Students will understand via performance the following concepts: line of scrimmage, scoring system, five running plays, five pass patterns, rules of touch football, defensive positioning, offensive positioning.

Then, using your own procedures, begin to teach the motor skills and combine these same skills with the aforementioned game concepts. Try to combine several of the motor skills and/or concepts into some form of game to promote interest or move toward the terminal game objective—regulation touch football.

Games analysis can be most helpful at this point for both the new and the experienced teacher. You can design new games or alter existing games to meet the needs of your students. One can find countless lead-up games that purport to promote certain motor skills development, but how many times have you found that these suggested games don't quite fit your situation? Simply adjust these games via the games analysis grid.

Let us now look at a very limited number of games designed via the games analysis approach.

TABLE 3-2.
CENTER PASS RELAY

Name of Game	Players	Equipment	Movement Pattern	Organizational Pattern	Limitations	Purpose
1. Center Pass Relay	5 - ? team	1 ball/team	Center pass, running	Each team is in column formation 5 ft. from one another.	The player must stay 5 ft. from another. The ball is centered from the first player to the next player. This continues until the last player receives the ball. He then runs to front of line, line moves back one player. First team to return to original start position is the winner.	1. To develop center pass skill. To promote team cooperation. To combine center pass with running the ball.

Now let's assume that something goes wrong with this particular game. For instance, the distance between players is causing the center pass to be bounced to the receiver. Simply shorten the distance between players. This sounds like a simple-minded answer that all of us know, but we have all known teachers who would not change anything in the game because "then one isn't playing the game the way it was meant to be played." Are we in physical education more interested in the outcome or in the process of skill development for all youngsters?

Let's carry the center pass relay one more step. Assume that even when the players are moved closer together many of them are still dropping the ball. Change the organizational pattern. Rather than having each team side by side, split the teams into the various geographical parts of the field or stagger the columns—both suggestions are shown below.

```
X   X X X X   X              X

X             X              X X

X             X     or       X X X

X   X X X X   X              X X X X

                             X X X

                             X X

                             X
```

Can you think of other organizational patterns? What does changing the organizational patterns do for the game? One thing it might do is begin to focus the attention upon each person's own team performance rather than worrying how well the other teams are doing. There are many alternatives to reduce team tension—can you think of some other changes? THERE IS MORE THAN ONE WAY TO PLAY A GAME.

So far we have looked at adjustment of one game designed to promote skill development of the center pass and running with the ball after it has been received. The following games show how a teacher can design even more games as lead-ups to the terminal objective.

TABLE 3-3.

Name of Game	Players	Equipment	Movement	Organ. Patterns	Limitations	Purpose
1. 6 man score	6/team	1 ball/team	running handoffs blocking	Each team's decision within limits described	Must have one center, one Q.B., one back, other three players you may position anywhere behind line of scrimmage. Only screen blocking allowed. May only use one play twice in succession, must use all five running plays you've designed. You have 8 plays to score a T.D. Field is 30-40 yds. long. Defensive 6 players must tag with 2 hands below the shoulders. Offsides not allowed, replay if this occurs. Six points for T.D., 3 points if defense prevents T.D. Game is over after each team of 6 has been on offense 3 times.	To develop 5 running plays. To learn initial rules of line of scrimmage, offsides two hand touch. To develop team play. To develop offensive and defensive concepts.
2. 6 man score w/pass	same as above	same as above	running catching passing	same as above	Same limits as above but this time you can only pass the ball. Defense must count to 5 before rushing the passer. If defense intercepts they may try to score on same play 6 pts. 1 point for each incomplete pass for defensive team.	Same as above with these additions: To develop pass plays, to develop offensive and defensive strategies vs. pass.

By changing the type of movement allowed in a game you have designed another game to fit the needs of the game purpose. Again, this concept is not unique, but it should point out to the teacher how one can develop a number of games from perhaps just one original game. It has been found advantageous to begin designing games by first describing the purpose of the game, then complete the other categories to meet the students' needs. With some practice a creative teacher can quite easily design lead-up games for almost any situation. The more a teacher performs this task the easier it becomes.

Finally, the type of game designed needs to reflect current growth and development information and current motor learning theory. It is not the purpose of this book to present a great wealth of growth and development information and then demonstrate how this information influences motor development. You will be shown how to use the games analysis grid to account for the various stages youngsters in elementary school go through. We will then deal primarily with visual perception as a developmental process.

When youngsters enter the first grade they possess an ability to track horizontally moving targets much more effectively than vertically moving objects. Therefore in primary grades, K-2, any game that requires visual tracking should be designed so that the performer only has to track on the horizontal plane. The next developmental stage, usually around grades 2-3, allows the youngsters to process information efficiently from vertically moving objects. Thus any game that now involves tracking could incorporate horizontal and vertical tracking. The ability to track a three-dimensional object through a variety of planes does not seem to appear until late grade 2 or grade 3. In addition, the ability to track an object through a variety of planes and move oneself to intercept the object does not seem to appear until grades 3-4. This is the reason why so many T-ball baseball players fail to catch a ball after running after a fly ball. This visual-perceptual information must be accounted for in the design of games that require tracking an object. The visual development of youngsters involves a process—a process implies moving from one condition to another. The age at which they go through this process is not the same for all youngsters. Some youngsters' visual-perceptual processes are quite mature at eight years of age while in others these processes mature much later. The fact that youngsters do not all develop at the same rate has dramatic implications for success in motor performance if a game is so structured that it does not consider the stage of development each youngster has reached. Certainly any game requiring visual tracking needs to account for the several developmental stages that each class of youngsters will exhibit. This is one reason for not playing too many team games with youngsters below grade 3. By the time grade 3 is reached many of the school age children are better able to handle game situations physically, emotionally, and socially.

According to Piaget (1965), Sutton-Smith (1971), and Loy and Inghan (1973), youngsters' ability to handle situations emotionally and socially also undergoes a developmental process. Helanko (1957) developed a table of socialization stages. For example, youngsters age 5-6 regard rules as sacred and absolute. These same youngsters exhibit a great deal of egocentric behavior. Thus to try to teach team games to this age group is most difficult, though possible. It is more important for this age group to experience a wealth of movement experiences. By ages 7-9, youngsters begin to exhibit cooperative behavior, and games rules need not be absolute. By the ages of 10-12 youngsters are capable of handling complex social interactions involving cooperation and competition. Rules are regarded as relative and solid group identities are being formed. Any game designed for middle and upper elementary school can begin to build into itself situations that promote cooperative behavior. Concurrently this is the age to deal with emotional and social reactions and conflicts that develop due to game design.

As mentioned in an earlier chapter, the game design may predispose itself to certain emotional and social conflicts. You, the teacher, must recognize what in a game is causing the inappropriate behavior. Is the game design too complex to allow for proper comprehension of the rules? Take the following example:

> I had a group of fourth and fifth graders who loved to play a rather complicated game of dodgeball. By design the game required subjective judgment on the part of the person throwing the ball as well as by the person getting hit by the ball. There was so much arguing and physical fighting that I had to stop the game. The youngsters were not able to "live up to the rules" and/or some honestly had no idea what the rules were. Changing a rule or two and focusing attention on the desired social and emotional behavior resulted in appropriate interaction. The process took four weeks.

This is a classic example of game design influencing social and emotional growth. As a teacher, you must recognize that too many rules within a game or too many components within any of the categories can lead to confusion on the part of the players. In asking a youngster to remember the structure of any given game you are assuming the possession of a most efficient short- and long-term auditory and visual memory. A limiting factor in poor gamesmanship on the part of the players is their failure to remember what they were supposed to do. Therefore, have each game build upon the previous one in terms of tasks one has to do and remember. Another cause for social sanctioning occurring in a game is subjective evaluation of rules by the participants. For example, youngsters called upon to evaluate subjectively whether or not they were tagged with two hands below the waist might lie about the results, depending on age and/or the major game outcome. If you haven't dealt with group interaction behavior then don't design a tournament where the top team receives some kind of reward. If you do, you are implying to the youngsters indirectly, by design, that the most important thing is to win rather than to understand the process of playing a game. A game purpose can be stated: learn how to cooperate, learn how rules affect group behavior, learn how to abide by the rules. Games designed to fulfill this purpose have been tried with fifth and sixth graders with resounding success. The following is an example:

A class of 35 fifth and sixth graders were given the objective of displaying (1) knowledge of the rules; (2) acceptance of subjective interpretation of the rules by opposing team members; (3) strategies to deal with opposing rule interpretations. Prior to playing a complex game of dodgeball, the entire class was taught how to display the three behavioral objectives mentioned. The game of dodgeball was designed so that the purpose of the game was to win by displaying the three desired behaviors.

Using a wrist counter, I viewed the game and kept "score" by counting each desired behavior when it occurred and recording it on a score sheet. After the game, we talked about the significance of the score. Having done this for several days, a student finally said, "Mr. Morris, it's not important what the score is cuz it's more fun to play the game without arguing—that's what we're learning, huh?"

The teacher's major role, then, is to examine the structure of the game and ascertain whether the structure is too complex to be internalized. If the youngsters can't make appropriate subjective interpretation of the rules don't design a game which mandates that this occur. In the case of the touch football game simply design the game so that the defense has to pull a flag off—this is objective and easily evaluated. Youngsters from grades 4-12 can learn how complex games can become. They can learn the relationship one category within a game has upon another category, and they can learn why rules are important. Often "cheating" in a game at the elementary school level is nothing more than forgetting a rule or never really understanding what the rule was in the first place. Have you had this occur?

Mike says, "Mr. Morris, John was cheating cuz he started before he was tagged!" Here's a solution to this problem—ask Mike to explain the rule to John. Focus the attention on Mike's explanation of the rule to John. What you are doing indirectly and very subtly is providing the class with a strategy to employ if they think someone is "cheating." The strategy is to reinforce the rule. If John chooses to break the rule the next time he plays the game, then say to him, "John, you indicated to me that you know the rule. Can I help you understand it? No? Well then, show me you know the rule."

More often than not John will no longer "cheat." If, however, he does break the rule, employ this strategy: "John, you have a choice to make—you may play the game demonstrating you know the rule or you can play the game and break the rule and then you get to sit out of the remaining games." John will now usually abide by the rule—if he doesn't you must follow through by saying, "John, I see *you* have decided to sit out." This way John accepts the responsibility for his behavior.

What is suggested here is that as a teacher you initially reinforce the rule, then reinforce the desired outcome because the youngsters may simply need to be re-cued as their auditory or visual memory may not have been functioning adequately. Finally give the youngsters realistic choices so that they have control over the play environment. This is one method to teach responsibility within a games lesson. Remember, one of our rules as educators is to help the child develop as a total human being and much can be learned within a games environment.

PROBLEM SOLVING VIA GAMES ANALYSIS

Problem solving is considered the highest level of intellectual development. It involves cognition in the identification, analysis, and solution of various problems. There are several kinds of problem solving behaviors. For example, a problem can be posed to the youngsters which require them to take apart the whole in order to better understand the parts. Another problem may require putting information together in an orderly manner to gain meaningful understanding of the newly formed whole. Quite another problem may simply be to identify that a problem exists within a given environment. Problems are constantly developing in physical education class and on the play field when youngsters are participating in games. For example, youngsters must constantly deal with analysis of the other teams weaknesses and/or strengths. They must be able to adapt to any change within their play environment so that they successfully cope with it.

Problem solving through games analysis as an approach within physical education requires both physical and cognitive involvement. A major consideration here is that the approach not only can provide opportunities for individuals to seek solutions to stated problems, but, more important, involves the student in the process of asking questions and *defining problems.* It is this unique characteristic of developing and cultivating the ability to independently discover and design new problems which is the essence of this approach.

A child meets daily demands and learns to cope with his environment more effectively through his ability to solve problems using certain logical operations. In this sense children as computers have become more efficient, that is, they are taught to carry out logical operations. But is it not equally important that they create problems, seek new possibilities, continually attempt to find a better question *as well as* a better answer for the questions already proposed? The physical education teacher is in an excellent position to provide the type of exhilarating and enthusiastic atmosphere which can foster this growth. Unfortunately, many of those who understand problem solving as a process have "intellectualized" themselves out of positions in which they might directly influence children and others. And those who can accomplish the most significant results with problem solving are usually not made aware of its potential and positive nature. Often physical educators are skeptical of introducing new ideas, not because they wish to maintain the status quo, not because the ideas are radical or difficult to introduce, but because the insertion of these different ideas may entail program shifts which in turn might offset more favorable aspects of the existent program.

An important consideration here is the ease with which a problem-solving approach can be included within the already existing physical education activities. When used in a games analysis situation problem solving can become as integral a part of a program as the teacher feels comfortable with. It can be an exciting aspect of any program and we would be naive to assume that if this is not accepted as an all-or-none commitment, it cannot be made to function effectively. It has merit whether offered as a total program or simply as an addition or augmentation to what already exists.

Before continuing it must be stressed that problem solving as introduced through games analysis is by no means a panacea for the many incongruities which exist between current educational theory and physical education as it is presently practiced in many public schools. It does not pretend to solve all problems nor does it claim to answer all questions. In fact, it may well raise more questions than answers. But if that is what learning is all about, then this should certainly be a step in the right direction. This approach is not meant to act as a replacement for other important facets of a program. It is a natural part of the learning process which assists the teacher in developing "self moving" individuals who are provided opportunities to search for, analyze, and attempt to solve problems related to game situations within their own range of physical and mental capabilities. It is, therefore, a positive contribution to the fostering of an inquisitive child who can more effectively explore and cope with his environment both physically and mentally.

The implications of such an approach are far-reaching. Everyone can experience success. Incorrect responses are not only never criticized but, in fact, do not even exist permitting all responses to serve, in some way, as a contribution to the basic learning situation. While not deliberately stressed, other behavioral variables such as self concept, confidence, cooperation among peers begin to emerge as by-products. Each individual is allowed to make decisions based upon self-evaluation, knowledge, skills and attitude; discipline becomes a minor consideration since both physical and mental efforts are constantly being focused on the subject matter.

By relinquishing an increasing number of decisions to the students regarding various aspects of the game situation, the teacher is established as a guide and is not expected to be continually providing correct answers. Much room is left open for creativity on the teacher's part. For example, being able to now pose challenging situations wherein the child can discover numerous problems may add that "extra" amount of excitement lacking in an otherwise adequate program. And finally, the teacher is not required to possess any special amounts of knowledge or high levels of performance ability.

The child who was heretofore labelled as atypical, clumsy or awkward may now be totally included and accepted as an equal since all abilities and all levels of ability are accounted for. Often the child who has the most to gain from games and physical activity programs is also the one who is most easily discouraged by these programs. But now, since all children are given opportunities to make major decisions on questions which were previously decided by others, such children find themselves easily challenged, willing to meet these challenges, and accepted on many more levels than before. The focus is no longer upon accepted standards of movement, but good ideas often become the more important aspect of various situations. Such children are sought for their ability to manipulate game components to accommodate their needs rather than their ability to perform according to predetermined arbitrary standards.

There are several ways to develop problem-solving activities within a games lesson. For many years this has occurred in the areas of gymnastics and dance in the form of movement education. In this approach the activities are less teacher-directed and more student-directed. More and more movement decisions are made by the student for the student rather than by the teacher. A new sense of freedom and responsibility is given to the student. Very few people have attempted to promote independent decision making in a game situation. Kirchner (1974), Maulden and Redfern (1970), and Mosston (1966) have suggested that problem solving and/or freedom to make decisions can also be accomplished in a games situation.

The following are a few specific ideas which you can use to introduce problem solving to your students in grades 3-12.

Utilizing the games analysis concept, you provide the students with a game framework which allows the youngsters to meet challenges of the game problem that you initially pose. Allowing youngsters this opportunity to investigate the large realm of solutions and design their game is of inestimable value to their intellectual and social development.

Youngsters in Grades 3-6

Divide the class of youngsters into reasonable working groups, perhaps three to five students per work group. Give each group three balls of various sizes, four hula hoops, and one beanbag. Pose the following problem to them: "Design a throwing, shooting game utilizing all of the equipment—every player must be engaged in the game at all times. In addition develop a rotation system so that everyone on the team gets to perform the game tasks. You have 8 minutes to design the game."

With this age group you need to circulate among all the groups providing necessary direction when it is called for. After a little time has passed, suggest to the groups that they try to play their game without waiting for the other groups to start. Within a very few minutes most of the groups will be performing. Often it is advisable to ask the youngsters to perform their game for the rest of the class. It is surprising how many solutions the youngsters come up with.

Another method of introducing problem solving to youngsters that has worked quite well is to take a game with which they are familiar and ask the whole class for solutions to this problem: "Within the game of prison dodgeball, change the method of moving around the court." Instantly the hands go up—some youngsters will suggest hopping, three-legged movements, skipping—the list is endless.

BASIC CONCEPT—pose a rather simple problem, preferably asking the youngsters to design a game with limited amounts of equipment, or ask them to change a category within a game they are familiar with. There are undoubtedly many other methods which will occur to you.

Students in Grades 7-12

Divide the class into teams of five to eight youngsters per team. Suggest to them that they must create a game ulitizing the equipment you are about to give them. Now you must prepare equipment boxes prior to class, one box for each team. Keep the number of individual pieces of equipment the same for all teams. Some of the following items have been included in these boxes: bowling pins, jump ropes, lummey sticks, wands, baseballs, footballs, basketball bladders, broken bats, and hula hoops. Each team's problem is to design a game that uses all of the equipment all of the time. Establish a time frame in which the students must complete this task. Again, you will be amazed at some of the games they design. A critical role you, the teacher, must play is to make sure that they consider safety factors in the use of all equipment.

Another method that has been used with this age group is the following: Having introduced the games analysis categories via discussion and visual description, make up a number of components for each category. Put the components into a hat (by category). Then ask each team (usually four to five teams of eight players) to send a representative up to pull four components out of the hat. After this is done for each category, each team's problem is to design a game using only the components drawn from the hat.

An example of the above procedure: Put into a hat movement components such as running, skipping, hopping, throwing. Each team picks the number of components specified and then designs a game. The most creative game receives some kind of reward. This method can be varied in many ways. For example, you can establish all the components for all of the categories but one. The students pick components from the hat for just that one category and must design a game using the given category components and the "picked-out-of-the-hat" components. One can increase the degree of difficulty of this problem-solving method by finally having the students pick all of the components for all of the categories. This, therefore, indicates a process is occurring within this problem-solving method. Again, the ability of the students to design these new games will surprise you. Indeed, the interest in physical education at the high school level seems to increase with the promotion of game design via problem solving. Each youngster now begins to share in the process of making a new game or a variation of one already known. Do you think that finding answers to problems that arise in designing a game and playing it with mutual consent is of value to students? Perhaps it is of more value to design your own game than to learn prestructured games with externally imposed rules year after year. You may discover more about your students as individual human beings than you ever thought possible.

A final method of introducing problem solving for this age group is to get the students to consider the feelings and capabilities of others. Pose this problem: Design a striking game (using given equipment) that mandates everyone is involved at the same time yet within the movement task each individual can choose how he wants the object delivered and each individual can have his choice of striking implement and size of object being struck." This is a more complicated problem that may require more guidance from you the teacher as well as more time in which to solve it. The reaction of many youngsters of various ages to this kind of problem has shown that they are forced to think about and account for other students' feelings and capabilities. It does require thinking and experimenting time—give it to them. Experience also shows that it is helpful to require the students to write out the game in a grid, accompanying the grid with a description of how to play the game. This suggests that the students bring pencils and paper to class—granted, an unheard-of behavior.

Certainly this last section utilizing problem solving implies that youngsters should be allowed to design creative games. It is through creative game design that students from grades 3 to 12 begin to understand the relationships among categories within a game structure. The students, at all grade levels, soon realize why it is necessary to have rules, how a change in one category affects the design of another category, how within a game there is a place for everyone's abilities, and, most importantly, how differences in ability make one feel good or bad about oneself. Kirchner (1974) suggests that youngsters in grades 3-6 be given initial problems guiding the movement tasks via a movement theme approach. The following chart is an attempt to summarize the kinds of experiences the teacher might consider in asking youngsters to create games.*

*Adapted from *Games Teaching* by E. Mauldon and H. B. Redfern (London: MacDonald and Evans, 1970).

Level 1, Age 8-9—Youngsters seem interested in participating on a group team whose objective is to beat another team—youngsters are still interested in enhancing their own individual skills—youngsters are interested in older children's games but accept readily modified versions—visual perceptual apparatus permits horizontal and vertical tracking of objects—movement control is satisfactory but they still may have difficulty in movement reactions to various movement situations. These youngsters are just learning to abide by rules and accept the judgment of others relative to rule attention.

Level 2, Age 10-12—Youngsters more interested in team play—they are able to concern themselves with the group (team) outcome; it is important that the "team" win—they more readily accept a code of rules governing the methods of play—additionally they exhibit a readiness to abide by subjective interpretations of the rules by other players or an external referee—the visual tracking apparatus is generally mature allowing for complex tracking capabilities. Movement control of body parts and the total body is much improved. They better react to changing game situations in movement sense. Physically they are stronger and consequently can perform more difficult movement tasks. They can understand inner workings of a game structure.

Level 3, Age 13-14—Youngsters are capable of abiding rules—they are also capable of understanding the structure of a game—this is the time to work on developing emotional and social growth within a game—due to puberty some movement capabilities are improved or altered, realize the effect this has upon their self concept within a game—they are concerned with precise rules strategies and tactics.

Level 4, Age 15-17—Students are capable of understanding emotions of others—they also want to exhibit precise skills within a game concept but they are most willing to perform problem solving activities within a game—highly creative if given the chance.

The preceding table is by no means complete. It is an attempt to summarize the necessary considerations teachers must realize when they design learning situations during a games lesson in physical education. Notice third grade is the lowest grade at which it is suggested you employ the games analysis concept. Piaget suggests forcing youngsters at too early an age into competitive situations may prove most damaging to their developing stages of understanding the nature and function of rules. Finally, remember that not all youngsters develop at the same rate; that is why it is important to learn how to change the games children play.

References

Helanko, R. pp. 238-47 *Personality and Social Systems,* ed. N.J. Smelser and W. T. Smelser. New York: Wiley, 1963 [article reprinted from *Acta Sociologica* 2 (1957): 229-40].

Kirchner, Glenn. Physical Education for Elementary School Children. Dubuque, Iowa: William C. Brown Co., 1974.

Loy, J.W., and Inghan, Alan G. "Play, Games and Sport in the Psychosocial Development of Children and Youth," pp. 257-306 in *Physical Activity,* ed. Lawrence Rarich. New York: Academic Press, 1973.

Loy, J.W., and Kenyon, G.S., eds. *Sports Culture and Society.* Englewood Cliffs, N.J.: Prentice-Hall, 1959.

Mauldon, E., and Redfern, H.B. *Games Teaching.* London: MacDonald and Evans, 1970.

Mosston, Muska. *Teaching Physical Education.* Columbus, Ohio: Charles E. Merrill Co., 1966.

Piaget, Jean. *The Moral Judgement of the Child.* New York: Free Press, 1965.

Sutton Smith, B. Paper delivered at 2nd World Symposium of Historical Sport and Physical Education, Banff, Alberta, Canada, 1971. Reprinted in *Physical Activity,* ed. Lawrence Rarich. New York: Academic Press, 1973.

Sutton-Smith, B., and Rosenberg, B.G. pp. 280-82 of Physical Activity, ed. Lawrence Rarich. New York: Academic Press, 1973 [article reprinted from *Journal of American Folklore* 74 (1961): 17-46].

Chapter

Methods of Presenting Games Analysis to Elementary and Secondary Youngsters

A more detailed discussion of how to introduce the games analysis concept into the schools seems to be called for at this point. It will, however, be a brief discussion since several ideas have already been presented in earlier chapters. Let us consider some ideas for instituting games analysis at the secondary level; these will be followed by some ideas for the elementary level.

SECONDARY

The concept can be introduced by either the direct or the indirect method. The following is a suggestion using the direct method:

> I simply lecture to the class explaining that each game is comprised of six categories. Within each category there are a number of components. Having defined a category and a component, I dissect a sport in which the group has demonstrated an interest and place its parts into the grid. I follow this up by asking the students how they could change the game by manipulating several of the components. The class is then asked to try out some of their suggestions by playing the game.

The indirect method involves a guided discovery approach, as in the following example:

I ask the students to tell me what kinds of things are found in all movement games. They proceed to tell me, and I write them on a blackboard. Next I ask the students to categorize the items listed on the board and, using guided discovery, I lead them to discover the categories found on the grid. Again, this is followed by the procedure used in the direct method as far as implementing the concept is concerned. This method takes a little more time, but seems to promote more initial interest and understanding of the concept.

Regardless of the method employed to introduce games analysis, it is suggested that you implement the concept while engaging in an activity that most of the students enjoy and understand. It is easier to change a part of a game that one already knows than it is to first learn a new game and then immediately change it.

ELEMENTARY

Although the games analysis concept can be used to design games for youngsters in grades 1 and 2, it is best not to involve them actively in the process. Beginning with grade 3, the following strategy has worked well:

In a similar approach to that used with secondary youngsters, I use a game with which the youngsters are familiar and ask them to suggest alternative movements within the stated game. The class tries the new movements and often this makes them realize that changing a movement may necessitate a change in the rules. After asking for several more alternatives in the movement category or the equipment category and actually playing these new versions, I sit the class down in front of a blackboard and dissect the just completed game into the appropriate categories on a G.A. grid. I change the names of the grid categories so that the youngsters understand the concept better. The new grid looks like the one shown on the next page.

The youngsters proceed to demonstrate that they know the concept of dissecting various games onto the grid. This is usually followed by gradually relinquishing decisions to the elementary youngsters as described earlier.

TABLE 4-1.

Name of Game	How Players Move	# of Players on a Team	Type of Equipment	Rules	Reasons for Playing the Game	What Group Pattern are Both Teams in During Game

I also try to make an analogy between the games analysis concept and remodeling a car. For example, "a car is made up of various parts like four wheels, steering wheel, motor, bumpers, etc. By changing a part of that car, rebuilding a 306 engine into a 350 engine, you have designed another type of car, but it is still a car. You can do the same with games—all games have these parts (pointing to grid)—by changing one part of the game you have designed another type of game, but it is still a game."

This approach has worked well over the last few years, along with some methods described in an earlier chapter. The main concern is to talk to the youngsters in terms they can understand. Use your discretion in applying the method that works best with your youngsters.

EXCEPTIONAL CHILDREN

It is particularly important to adapt games to meet the skill level of youngsters who are mentally retarded or physically handicapped. Quite often one can find no ready designed games that meet the developmental needs of these youngsters. The games analysis concept can be applied in two ways to meet these needs:
1. Develop and design games that enhance the motor abilities of all the participants.
2. Ask the youngsters to modify existing games.
The following is an example:

We have played a form of floor hockey with the wheel-chair handicapped. The youngsters were each given a pole which they could manipulate and which functioned as the hockey stick. A gigantic balloon became the puck, and the youngsters were asked to move the balloon toward the opposing team's goal, a hanging gymnastic mat. Special rules were made by the youngsters, and they showed excitement, interest, and ability. When the youngsters were asked for suggestions to alter the game to meet everyone's needs some of them offered the following suggestions:
add another ball into the game;
the stick can only be used in one hand;
have more than one goal;

> if the puck hits the large goal it is worth 2 points; if it hits the smaller goal if is worth 4 points.
>
> The students began to design games taking the physical limitations of others into consideration.

Youngsters whose developmental handicap is only mild or moderate can also adapt and design games. The same procedures used with developmentally sound students are used. The process may be a little slower and it may be necessary to change some terms to fit the situation, but these students are perfectly capable of performing the games analysis concept. It is most gratifying to begin to see certain problem-solving behaviors develop as you ask the students to design more and more games. You may have to begin the games analysis process by providing them with alternatives from which to choose. The following is an example:

> Let's say that the students are playing a form of basketball. Say to them, "In this game you have moved the ball by dribbling with your hand. Here are three other ways to move the ball—carry it, kick it, air dribble it (demonstrate this one). You must now choose one of those three ways to move the ball—which shall it be?" Play the game for a few minutes, stop it, and now ask them if they have any more ideas on how to move the ball. Pick one or two of the ideas and play the new version. The youngsters are now well on their way to utilizing this concept.

It is important that the developmentally handicapped be given opportunities to think as well as strategies to employ within a certain situation. Because movement is fun, make use of this fact and begin to provide these students with strategies and appropriate movement tasks which will enhance motor efficiency.

This has been a brief attempt to demonstrate a few methods of introducing the games analysis concept. There are other methods which you will devise as you work with this concept. The information provided to you thus far comprises:

1. Rationale for games analysis concept.
2. Explanation of the concept.
3. Uses of the concept.
4. How to implement the concept.
5. Explanation of the concept's educational value.

All of this presupposes that you, the reader, have information available to you regarding what should be taught, observation techniques for youngsters using the concept, and an assessment tool to measure movement competency. The next chapter provides limited information for the preceding suppositions.

Chapter

Observation
and Assessment
Alternatives

Consistent with the philosophy of games analysis, it is important to be able to observe youngsters at play while looking for specific types of physical behavior. If it is important to consider the individual abilities of youngsters in a game environment, then one needs to observe and assess the movement of each individual. This suggests that the youngsters only need to know how they are doing individually, i.e., relative to themselves rather than in comparison to group norms.

Two new concepts relative to observation and evaluation procedures employed in an elementary physical education setting are therefore presented. Learning to control individual body parts, body segments, and then the entire body is a prerequisite to efficient movement behavior. Concern yourself with how much body and movement control each child exhibits while jumping and running rather than with how far one youngster jumped or how fast another can run 40 yards. If youngsters can initially demonstrate control of their movements, then movement for maximum performance (how fast, how far) will be greatly enhanced over time. Because youngsters display a maximum performance in a given movement behavior this does not necessarily provide information relative to the mechanical efficiency of their movement patterns. They may be performing a skill in a significantly incorrect, i.e., mechanically inefficient, manner which affects performance. By changing the mechanical inefficiency you might be able to improve the child's total movement capability.

For years in physical education we have administered tests which measure performance. Examples of items on these tests are: number of sit-ups performed in 30 seconds, number of pull-ups, number of laps run in 12 minutes. The reason we do this is quite simple—it is easy to measure and record this type of information. This information does not necessarily allow the teacher to understand how or why a youngster moves in a particular manner. If we profess to care about individual development and if we profess to teach the individual, then we need a method of observing and evaluating individual performance in terms of motor control quality rather than maximum performance quantity. To do this the teacher must be provided with techniques for observing a youngster for motor control. This requires a radical shift in thinking and observation technique.

The first step is to look at the individual performers as separate entities rather than observe the product of their movement. For example, observe a youngster's total bodily movements while throwing a ball rather than observing where the ball was thrown. Look at the youngster's total bodily movements while performing a lay-up in basketball rather than observing whether or not the ball went in the hoop. In order to help youngsters improve their skill performance you must be able to provide them with adequate sound directions that will allow the youngsters to make adjustment in their movement behavior in order that the ball go through the hoop. Does the coach who yells "Try harder, hang in there!" provide the performer with adequate information that will produce a better performance next time? This strategy of observing the performer rather than the performance outcome is difficult to learn, and it does take time. However, with constant reminders to yourself, the strategy can be developed. Once this has occurred it is time to move to the next step.

The second step is to begin to observe the individual body parts rather than the total movement of the body. Observe general body segments and then the individual body part. For example, when a youngster is beginning to learn how to throw a ball efficiently look at the lower body segment (waist to feet). Specifically identify which foot the youngster is stepping forward with. Arm-leg opposition should be exhibited—step forward with left leg if throwing right-handed.

It is far more important to observe what a youngster is currently doing in a movement task than to concentrate attention and advice on what is *not* being done. The reason for this is that the teacher first needs to understand what the performer is able to do in order to be able to identify where the youngster is on the developmental sequence within the skill and finally prescribe the next movement task. This presupposes that each teacher knows the developmental sequences of the basic motor patterns, e.g., throwing, catching, kicking, jumping, running, striking. It is not the purpose of this book to provide that information, but it is suggested that all interested teachers examine Ralph Wickstrom's *Fundamental Motor Patterns* (1970) for further information.

Now that we possess the strategies to observe youngsters' ability to control their movement patterns, let us apply the concept to the motor patterns of throwing and the standing long jump.

THROWING

First look at the entire movement pattern, and then look at the legs in relation to the youngster's throwing arm. Many first and second graders will step forward with the foot on the same side as the throwing arm, i.e., right foot forward, right-handed thrower. This is an immature pattern of throwing, so simply tell the youngster to step forward with the left foot next time. Also watch how close to or far away from the head the ball is held when the arm is cocked, i.e., brought back prior to throwing the ball. The ball should be close to the head in order to control it. Look at the youngster's hips and shoulders. Both body parts should rotate away from the target or to the right side with the shoulders rotating 1½ times the distance the hips rotate. Have any youngster who is not doing this practice rotating the hips and shoulders first without the ball and then with the ball.

STANDING LONG JUMP

First look at the youngster's entire bodily movement pattern. Next look at the feet. It is common to see youngsters move their feet to a stagger position just before jumping—this is inefficient. Tell them to keep both feet still before jumping. Next the youngsters' arms as they prepare to jump and also during the jump. Many youngsters will not swing their arms like a pendulum to provide arm force—they simply let their arms dangle at their sides. They can play an arm swinging game just to get them swinging the arms—don't let them jump. After a few trials in which they demonstrate their swinging ability let them perform the whole task of jumping.

The above remarks did not cover all of the body parts that you as a teacher should watch, but the few instances given should enable you to begin observing youngsters' performance critically and from the point of view of motor control. One last comment should perhaps be made relative to motor control, and that is that the structure of the task we ask youngsters to do dramatically dictates whether they will exhibit the kind of movement pattern desired. Take the following example:

If you want a youngster to exhibit a mature throwing pattern, ask him to throw a ball against a wall rather than to play catch with a partner standing 6 feet away. In asking the youngster to perform the latter task you are really telling him to get the ball to his partner so that she doesn't drop it. Thus he will throw in the best way he knows to get the ball to his partner.

This concept has implications for use of equipment. It would be too rough on school walls to have the children throw hard type balls, so simply use nylon balls, i.e., balls made from nylons, to throw against the wall. In addition these nylon balls won't bounce a half-mile away from the children, so they can spend most of their time practicing throwing rather than practicing retrieving.

If you don't want the standing long jumper to exhibit an inefficient jumping pattern, eliminate how far she jumps until she can perform the task under control.

Finally, if you want a youngster to practice just the action of kicking, use half-gallon milk cartons. Ask the children to kick the milk carton rather than a ball. Have you ever kept track of the time a youngster spends in retrieving a ball that he has kicked versus the amount of time spent on kicking? This again is a classic example of how the structure of a task affects motor outcome, specifically retrieval versus movement time. Movement time is nothing more than the time you allow a youngster to move or practice a task.

ASSESSMENT TOOL

Observation strategies have been presented, but it is now important to discuss how you will discover whether you are doing what you think you are doing with the youngsters. This falls within the area of assessment.

Assessment should be used for diagnosis and prescription of movement behavior, and for nothing else. An assessment tool should provide you with information which identifies why a youngster is behaving in a certain way, and from this you should be able to provide the students with helpful information so that they can improve their motor performance.

Games can provide movement experiences that aid in the development of motor skills. In order to develop the motor skills within a game framework, one must structure the game appropriately, which means that one must be able to identify the factors that influence the development of that skill and present the movement tasks in parts that each learner can reasonably cope with. Thus a use of the games analysis grid is to design a series of games adopting a task and factor analysis format. We will examine the factor analysis concept as it is applied to game design.

Let us examine the motor behavior of striking in terms of the factors that seem to influence its level of performance by elementary students. The chart on the next page (Table 5-1) identifies several, but not all, of these factors.

The chart shows some of the factors identified as affecting the motor performance of striking. Within each factor a degree of difficulty continuum has been established from easy to more difficult as the directional arrows indicate. For example, after analyzing the striking implement factor, research and experience have shown that it is easiest to strike an object with one's hand. It is a bit more difficult to strike an object with a paddle and most difficult to strike it with a bat. Research by Bruce (1966) and Williams (1968) suggests that youngsters can first visually track a horizontally moving object, then they can track a vertically moving object, and finally, around age nine or ten, most youngsters can efficiently track an object travelling through a variety of planes or in an arc. It is suggested that a larger object is easier to strike than a small object when first learning this motor behavior. Available research also indicates that it is easier to strike an object that travels to your perferred side than one that travels to your nonpreferred side. An object travelling directly at the performer is the most difficult to strike. Moran (1975) recently completed a study indicating that the ball color influenced the ability of elementary youngsters to exhibit efficient striking behavior. He found that the youngsters were able to strike the blue balls best, then yellow, and finally white balls. When designing a movement task you definitely should consider the visibility of the object, and the ball

TABLE 5-1

Striking Implement	Trajectory of Object Being Struck	Size of Object Being Struck	Object Direction in Flight	Weight of Object Being Struck	Color of Object Being Struck	Anticipation Location	Speed Object is Travelling
Hand	Horizontal	Large	Right	Light	Blue	How far must the performer move before striking the object	Slow
↓	↓	↓	↓	↓	↓		↓
Paddle	Vertical	Small	Left	Heavy	Yellow		Fast
↓	↓		↓		↓		
Bat	Arc		Center		White		

color and background seem to influence the efficiency of the striking action. The closer the object is to the performer the easier it is for him to strike it and efficiency of striking decreases the farther the object is away from the performer. Most of the preceding information is nothing more than common sense which recently has been supported by research. A teacher can now design movement tasks and games that allow each task and game to account for current stages of motor development by the students. The ability to account or identify what stage each student is at suggests that there exists a procedure for assessing these stages. A simple assessment tool called a movement profile sheet indicates what each student's ability is within a single factor or any combination of striking factors. Below is a sample motor profile (Table 5-2) sheet that has analyzed and demonstrated the striking ability a student has exhibited while considering the interaction of two factors—striking implement and size of the object being struck.

TABLE 5-2

	S_1	S_2	S_3	S_4
I_1	Succeeded on 1-8-76	Succeeded on 1-9-76	Succeeded on 1-17-76	Succeeded on 1-23-76
I_2	Tried but failed 1-8-76	Succeeded on 1-10-76	Succeeded on 1-22-76	Failed on 1-23-76
I_3	Tried but failed 1-8-76	Tried but failed 1-10-76	Tried but failed 1-22-76	Failed on 1-23-76
I_4				Failed on 1-23-76

S = size of object	I = striking implement
S_1 = 12" balloon	I_1 = hand
S_2 = 10" plastic beach ball	I_2 = paddle
S_3 = 8" rubber ball	I_3 = racquet
S_4 = 4" rubber ball	I_4 = whiffle bat

The profile sheet on the opposite page is easier to read if you only put the date in the appropriate space upon successful completion of the task, as demonstrated.

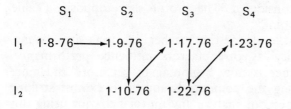

The teacher establishes the criteria for successful completion of the task. For example, in Box S_1, I_1, the criteria might be: "Hit a 12″ balloon with your hand in a forward direction three times in succession." It is up to you to decide upon the criteria to assess successful completion of the task. Try not to influence the task by adding the influence of yet another factor. This profile sheet also indicates to the teacher which of the two factors under investigation influenced this particular student's striking ability. Which factor was it—size of the object or striking implement? By observation, the striking implement seems to be the more limiting factor of the two simply because the student was able to strike all the sizes of the object but could only strike with a hand or a paddle. This information is important for the teacher because now the teacher knows why a student demonstrates a particular kind of motor performance. Thus in a game form this particular student should be allowed to use a hand or a paddle to strike with. More than likely if she uses a bat she will not be successful.

Another service the profile sheet provides is that it gives the teacher specific directions in which to go in designing motor tasks. Knowing the student's current motor status and the factor or factors influencing successful performance, the teacher should now be able to help him improve his motor performance. Having been given appropriate tasks, the student should improve in his ability to perform. When assessing a motor skill, the teacher needs to account for all the factor interactions rather than just settling for a two-factor interaction, i.e., it would be appropriate to investigate the student's striking ability when one, two, or three other factors are considered. The profile sheet opposite (Table 5-4) illustrates the point.

With such a profile sheet, the teacher can look at a youngster's striking ability as three factors influence performance. Moreover, the teacher is now beginning to get more and more information regarding the youngster's ability to exhibit striking behavior. The teacher can analyze any motor behavior using this concept and can choose to identify as many of the factors that influence the specific motor behavior as seem necessary. This new assessment technique presupposes that: (a) one is able to identify the factors that influence a motor behavior; (b) one is able to design movement tasks within each factor on an easy to more difficult continuum; (c) one has a variety of equipment; and (d) one knows the classroom mechanics of administering the concept.

To illustrate the above, the following is a personal identification of the factors that seem to affect the motor behaviors of striking, catching, kicking, and throwing:

1. Size of object;
2. Color of object;
3. Trajectory of object;
4. Weight of object;
5. Speed of object;
6. Color of background;
7. Anticipation location;
8. Texture of object;
9. Illumination level;
10. Illumination type;
11. Object direction in flight relative to performer;
12. Speed of performance by student.

There are undoubtedly many more factors that can be identified, but they must be left for another book. Most of the above-mentioned factors do not affect throwing although Nos. 1 and 3 (being thrown), 4 and 5 (speed of object being thrown), 8 and 12 seem to influence the throwing behavior. The color of a ball and background affecting the skill of catching is supported by Morris (1974) in recent research where blue, yellow, and white balls against a black, white background produced the best catching results in the order listed. Both Morris and Moran (1975) have suggested that more research be done in this area of object visibility. In the near future, therefore, it should be possible to

TABLE 5-4

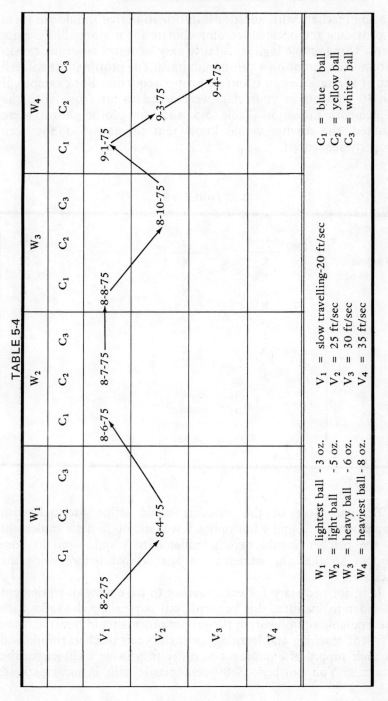

W_1 = lightest ball - 3 oz.
W_2 = light ball - 5 oz.
W_3 = heavy ball - 6 oz.
W_4 = heaviest ball - 8 oz.

V_1 = slow travelling-20 ft/sec
V_2 = 25 ft/sec
V_3 = 30 ft/sec
V_4 = 35 ft/sec

C_1 = blue ball
C_2 = yellow ball
C_3 = white ball

provide teachers with additional information that should aid them in providing the optimal learning climate for motor skill development. Using simple logic, it is fairly easy to design movement tasks within each factor on a continuum basis. The profile sheet will tell you if the task design is out of proper sequence. For example, if the 30 students in your class were asked to hit a ball with the implements shown in Table 5-5 and the profile shown there resulted, the teacher would know that the task had not been properly sequenced.

TABLE 5-5

Student		I_1	I_2	I_3	I_4
	1	X	X	X	X
	2	X	X	X	X
	3	X	X	X	X
	4	X	X		X
	5	X	X		X
	6	X	X		X
	7	X	X		X
	8	X	X		

I_1 = hand
I_2 = paddle
I_3 = racquet
I_4 = fat bat

Because most of the students could strike the ball with implements 1, 2, and 4 but only a few could do so with implement 3, the teacher should switch implements 3 and 4 on the continuum so that the students use the fat bat before using the racquet.

It is not necessary for each teacher to have a lot of equipment in order to institute this concept, but sequencing the tasks with the available equipment, in the proper order, should result in more efficient teaching and learning. Over the years teachers should add to their supply of equipment in order to provide a choice for the students. You can buy 59-89 cent plastic balls in supermarkets, save the bladders of old, worn-out basketballs, keep the broken bats, racquets, and broom handles. All of these items can provide you with graduated equipment that allows each student to start with tasks that are easy and proceed developmentally to more difficult tasks.

Administration of the motor profile is quite simple. Each teacher can administer the assessment concept either in groups or individually. Provide a station or stations that assess specific performance in your own gym. The youngsters can administer the task for the specific motor behavior either individually or in a group. With third and fourth graders, fifth and sixth graders can be used as the assessors at these assessment stations. Parents, other teachers, or the youngsters themselves can self-administer the tasks in the upper grades. They must be taught the task administration procedures and the teacher must develop an environment of mutual trust in the gym if self-administration is to work. Experience has shown that youngsters will not be dishonest if they are given the opportunity to demonstrate honest behavior. The learning environment that requires individual analysis rather than individual comparison to group standing will promote a positive response to self-administration of the profile sheet. Because the motor profile concept is, by design, concerned with each individual's performance rather than with a comparative-position performance (individual's placement relative to group) it lends itself to the exhibition of honest behavior by students.

It is, however, important not to misuse this concept. We would be defeating the profile's purpose if we were to attempt to attach a letter grade to a youngster's performance within the profile sheet. The profile is intended to state each individual's current movement status, assessing the factors that most affect each individual's performance and offering direction for the teaching of the motor behavior. The profile concept is for the individual and concerns itself with the individual's progress. The following example illustrates how a teacher or administrator can misuse the motor profile assessment concept.

A teacher is teaching the skill of throwing to his class. The assessment tool is similar to the tool mentioned previously in the text. He is presently assessing the influence of two factors upon the skill of throwing. He makes the following remark: "If you can perform the task at L_3, B_4 you will get an A+. Likewise successful performance of L_1, B_3 gets you an A-;

dependent upon what box you end up in, this determines your grade."

	L_1	L_2	L_3	L_4
B_1		C		C^+
B_2	B–	B		B^+
B_3	A–		A	
B_4			A^+	

This example represents *MISUSE* of the concept. It is not important to get a letter grade because the grade does not account for growth data, factor analysis data, etc. The teacher wants to know where the student is as an individual. Please, therefore, don't misuse the concept.

Another way to misuse this concept is to stop evaluating the factors that affect motor performance. One needs to continue to keep abreast of current research that suggests the relationship certain factors have with competent performance of basic movement behaviors. Teachers should also evaluate their factor analysis progressions within tasks in order to make sure that the tasks presented are actually aiding the performer.

Games analysis can incorporate the task analysis concept quite easily. A teacher can design a series of games that provides for progressive improvement in selected motor behaviors by focusing upon one, two, three or more factors that influence said motor behaviors.

EXAMPLE: You want to enhance the development of catching and kicking skills in your class. Each youngster works individually to develop motor competency in catching and kicking and they now are ready to use these skills in a game form. As the teacher you have identified certain factors that affect the performance of these two skills. (See Table 5-6.)

Movement profiles have been established for both motor skills which look at only two factors at a time. (See p. 64.)

TABLE 5-6.
KICKING FACTORS

Size of Object	Foot used to Kick	Weight of Object	Type of Kick used	Speed of Object	Shape of Object
Large → Small	Preferred → Non-Preferred	Light → Heavy	Toe → Instep	Stationary → Slow → Fast	Round → Oblong

CATCHING FACTORS

Color of Ball	Angle of Trajection	Size of Object	Speed of Object	Weight of Object	Texture of Object Being Caught
Blue → Yellow → White	Horizontal → Vertical → Arc	Large → Small	Slow → Fast	Light → Heavy	Soft → Hard

KICKING PROFILE SHEET

Size of Object (S)   Weight of Object (W)

Easy - Difficult

	S_1	S_2	S_3	S_4
Easy W_1				
W_2				
W_3				
W_4				

Difficult

W_1 = 6 oz. ball	S_1 = largest ball - 18" diameter
W_2 = 8 oz. ball	S_2 = large ball - 14" diameter
W_3 = 12 oz. ball	S_3 = small ball - 12" diameter
W_4 = 16 oz. ball	S_4 = smallest ball - 8" diameter

CATCHING PROFILE SHEET

Texture of Object (T)   Angle of Trajection (A)

Easy ⟶ Difficult

	T_1	T_2	T_3	T_4
A_1				
A_2				
A_3				

T_1 = fleece ball	A_1 = horizontal plane
T_2 = nerf ball	A_2 = vertical plane
T_3 = nylon ball	A_3 = ball travels in arc
T_4 = whiffle ball	

TABLE 5-7
GAME GRID

Game	Players	Organ. Pattern	Equipment	Movement	Limitations	Purpose
1	3/team	Random	*Kicking-S_1 W_1 Catching-T_1	Kicking-Toe Kick Catching-A_1	Teacher Designed	Develop Catching and Kicking Skills
2			Kicking-S_2 W_2 Catching-T_2	Kicking-Same Catching-A_2		
3			Kicking-S_2 W_3 Catching-T_3	Kicking-Same Catching-A_3		
4			Kicking-S_3 W_3 Catching-T_4	Kicking-Same Catching-A_3		
5			Kicking-S_3 W_4 Catching-T_4	Kicking-Same Catching-A_3		

*Refer to profile sheets on page 64

TABLE 5-7 ILLUSTRATES HOW TO APPLY THE MOTOR PROFILE INFORMATION TO THE GAMES ANALYSIS GRID.

> Having done all of the preceding you either design games or adapt current games so that you progressively allow the preceding factors to dominate the game design.

You have now, with each new game, built upon the previous game's factors. Table 5-7 is only an example. You, of course, will adjust the game design to meet the individual's needs. In addition, you could design into each game several other factors that influence the skills being worked on. Simply by referring to the youngsters' profile sheets you can design games appropriate to their movement needs and capabilities.

Let's look at a typical fifth grader's profile sheet and then design a game utilizing the information on the sheet. For the sake of the discussion our fifth grader will be named Lisa. Again, let's look at the skills of catching and kicking and specifically analyze only two factors that affect each of the motor skills.

CATCHING PROFILE SHEET

Texture of Object (T)   Angle of Trajection (A)

Easy ──────────────────→ Difficult

NAME___Lisa_____

	T_1	T_2	T_3	T_4
A_1	10-2			
A_2		10-10		
A_3			11-2	11-8

T_1 = fleece ball A_1 = horizontal plane
T_2 = nerf ball A_2 = vertical plane
T_3 = nylon ball A_3 = ball travels in arc
T_4 = whiffle ball

KICKING PROFILE SHEET

Size of Object (S)   Weight of Object (W)

Easy ──────────→ Difficult

NAME Lisa

	S_1	S_2	S_3	S_4
W_1	10-2			
W_2		10-10		
W_3			11-2	11-8
W_4				

W_1 = 6 oz. ball	S_1 = largest ball - 18" diameter
W_2 = 8 oz. ball	S_2 = large ball - 14" diameter
W_3 = 12 oz. ball	S_3 = small ball - 12" diameter
W_4 = 16 oz. ball	S_4 = smallest ball - 8" diameter

The dates in each profile sheet represent the dates Lisa successfully completed the appropriate movement task. Both Lisa and the teacher know what Lisa is capable of doing when she is asked to kick or catch a ball. The teacher can now design a game that will enhance development of these skills to meet Lisa's needs. Using the games analysis grid, here's what a game might look like using the information garnered from the motor profile sheets. (See Table 5-8.)

Description:

Batting Team—The batting team is up for only 2 minutes, then they go to the field. The batting team divides into two groups of four players with one group at bat at a time—the

TABLE 5-8

Name of Game	Players	Organ. Pattern	Equipment	Movement	Limitations	Purpose
Kick and Go	8/team	Random in field- hula hoops in circle	kicking ball of choice- catching ball of choice	kicking catching running throwing	1. Kick ball of choice into field. 2. Run as group of 4 around all 7 bases before fielding team completes task. 3. Fielding team must have one person re- trieve kicked ball, place in hula hoop at center of field. 4. Once this is done, all other fielding players stand inside hoop, pick up ball and play self catch for 7 catches—ball must go above shoulders. 5. Complete this task before runners cross the home plate for out. 6. Time limit game— batting team up for 2 minutes only.	To develop kicking and catching skills.

groups alternate batting. One player in the group kicks the ball rolled by the teacher; this player, along with the other three group members, runs around all the seven bases and returns to home base. If the last member of the batting group crosses home plate before the fielding team completes its task, they score one run. Then the next group bats.

Fielding Team—Players start outside their hula hoops. Once the ball is kicked, the player closest to the kicked ball retrieves it and returns it to a hula hoop found in the center of the field. Once this is accomplished, all the fielding players stand inside their own hula hoops, pick up their balls, and play vertical catch seven times with themselves. The ball must go above their shoulders. If they can do all of this before the last person in the batting group crosses home plate then an out is registered. After 2 minutes time, the two teams switch places.

Lisa would have her choice of balls to kick, one that she is capable of kicking, and likewise she would have her own ball to play catch with when she is out in the field. Each of these balls would change from 10-2 to 11-8 within this particular game. This then is an example of how games analysis can make use of information provided by movement profile sheets.

This idea may suggest to some that a lot of time be spent in preparing lessons and also that it is necessary to have a lot of equipment. Again, use the equipment you now have, attempt to get more, and start designing movement profile sheets and alternative games. It takes only a few hours to design profile sheets, put them on a stencil, and run off several dozen. Only attempt to use this concept initially with maybe one sport or just a couple of motor skills. Slowly over the weeks and months expand the concept to other movement areas or games. If you believe that the motor development of your students is important you will spend the extra minutes to become a precision movement teacher. Remember, there is nothing sacred about the game design Lisa played. As a matter of fact, there are many more versions of the game the youngsters could be asked to play. Likewise, there is nothing sacred about the number of choices allowed for each identified factor affecting a motor behavior. Although $S_1 - S_4$ and $W_1 - W_4$' choices were shown in the kicking profile sheet, there are obviously more choices available—it all depends on the type and amount of equipment you have.

Finally, in the appendix at the back of this book there are a number of examples of choices allowed for several factors that affect performance of selected motor behaviors. Remember that they are examples and should by no means be regarded as complete.

References

Bruce, Russell. "The Effects of Variations in Ball Trajectory upon the Catching Performance of Elementary School Children." Ph.D. dissertation, University of Wisconsin, 1966.

Keogh, Jack. Section entitled "Development in Fundamental Motor Tasks" in *A Textbook of Motor Development* by Charles B. Corbin. Dubuque, Iowa: Wm. C. Brown, 1973.

Moran, Gary. "The Effect of Ball Color and Background Color on the Striking Performance of Second, Fourth, and Sixth Grade Children." Ph.D. dissertation, University of Oregon, 1975.

Morris, Gordon S. "The Effects Ball Color and Background Color Have upon the Catching Performance of Second, Fourth, and Sixth Grade Youngsters." Ph.D. dissertation, University of Oregon, 1974.

Morris, Gordon S. "Equipment Color: A Limiting Factor." *JOHPER* 46 (June 1975):8.

Wickstrom, Ralph. *Fundamental Motor Patterns.* Philadelphia: Lea and Febiger, 1970.

Williams, Harriet. "The Effects of Systemic Variation of Speed and Direction of Object Flight and of Skill and Age Classification upon Visuoperceptual Judgement of Moving Object in Three-dimensional Space." Ph.D. dissertation, University of Wisconsin, 1968.

Chapter

Examples of Games Designed for Specific Movement Areas

This chapter will provide the reader with examples of games from which it is hoped more games will be designed to meet the needs of developing children. All of the games presented have been either played or designed by the youngsters themselves. The format of this chapter will be as follows:

1. Sections on softball, volleyball, basketball, tag, and relay games.
2. Within these sections, where appropriate, games for elementary school students and secondary students will be presented.

The order of game presentation does not reflect any progression in terms of development—the games are simply representative of the hundreds of games developed during the past seven years by either the writer or his students.

SOFTBALL TYPE GAMES

In designing a game of this type you must remember that the visual-perception system may influence the kinds of movements a youngster is capable of performing. You will notice in most of the softball games that movements other than those which are an integral part of the game are included within the game structure.

Remember, you can substitute or alter any component within the structure of these games. By simply changing the major movement task from hitting to kicking you have developed seven
(go to page 83)

GAME 6-1. WORKUP (ELEMENTARY)

Players	Equipment	Movements	Organ. Pattern	Limitations	Purpose
1 - 8 can be played with as few as 3 players	bat, balls of various types	hitting, running, fielding, catching, bowling	somewhat random—1 batter—1 pitcher—rest are fielders	1. Batter stays at bat until a fielding player hits the bat on ground or until a fielder catches a fly ball. 2. Batting rotation follows: current batter, upon an out, moves to outfield, pitcher moves to batter, a fielder moves to pitcher. 3. If batter can catch the ball after it hits the bat but before the ball hits the ground he remains at bat. 4. Upon successful catch of a fly ball, the catcher changes places with the batter and the batter assumes the fielders position in the rotation.	To develop fielding and tracking skills.

Description: A batter hits the ball toward the fielders. He then places the bat on the ground. The fielder rolls the ball toward the bat, if he hits it, then everyone moves up one position. If he doesn't, the batter continues hitting the ball.

GAME 6-2. ONE BASE (ELEMENTARY)

Players	Equipment	Movements	Organ. Pattern	Limitations	Purpose
2 team 5-10 per team	bat, balls, one base	hitting, fielding, running, throwing, and catching	X - players O - base - home plate - - - thrown bat boundaries	1. Two outs/inning or 5 run limit, then teams switch positions. 2. Teacher is pitcher. 3. Stay at bat until batter hits ball—fair ball anywhere ball is hit. 4. To get an out you must: (a) catch a fly or catch a ball after one bounce (b) tag runner out with ball (c) get ball to base before runner gets to base. 5. Thrown bat by hitter outside boundaries is an out. 6. Runner may stay at base, return upon next hit. 7. Base is 30' - 40' from home plate.	To develop basic softball skills plus introduce base running strategies.

Description: This game is similar to regular softball except it has only one base quite a distance from home plate. The batting team, one member at a time, goes to bat until batter hits the ball. Batter runs to the base, either stays or returns—depends on the situation. To score a run the batter must return to home plate and touch it. The fielders play in the field like in regulation softball. When 2 outs or 5 runs are scored, the teams trade jobs. Play as long as you like.

GAME 6-3. MAGLADRY BALL (ELEMENTARY)

Players	Equipment	Movements	Organ. Pattern	Purpose
4-12/ team	1 batting tee, 4 bowling pins, hula hoop for each fielder, 3 different types of balls	running, hitting, bowling, catching, throwing		To develop running, hitting, bowling, catching, throwing skills. To promote team strategy.

Limitations:

1. Time limit game—batting team line up for 1-1/2 mins. only.

2. How to make an out: the only way to make an out is to perform specific tasks as fielders, get on special ball to out plate before batter crosses home.

3. Batter's job: hit plastic ball off of batting tee, run to bowling pin area. Stay behind line (10' from pins) and bowl a ball until all pins are knocked over. Then run to home plate.

4. Fielders: after batter hits the ball, one player retrieves the ball, rest of players stand inside hoop—throw the retrieved ball to 7 different players—if the ball is dropped, start the count all over again—person receiving the 7th throw runs to the center hoop and places the ball inside the out hoop—it must stay in the hoop—if all of this is done before batter crosses home, the batter is out!

GAME 6-4. MAGLADRY BALL PLUS (ELEMENTARY)

Players	Equipment	Movements	Organ. Pattern	Purpose
same as game 6-3	same as game 6-3 except no bowling equipment need several more hula hoops	same as game 6-3		same as game 6-3

—go thru hoop

—home

—out hoop

Limitations:

1. Same as game 6-3.
2. Same as game 6-3.
3. Batter's job: hit plastic ball off batting tee, batter runs to "go thru hoop" (15'-20' from batting tee), holds hoop perpendicular to floor—rest of teammates must run through the hoop; all these players must then run and cross home plate.
4. Fielder's job: same as game 6-3 except the player receiving the 7th throw simply runs the ball to the out hoop.
5. If the fielding team gets the ball to the out hoop before everyone on the batting team has crossed home plate, an out is registered.

Description: The limit category describes this game and game #3 quite adequately. By designing the game in this manner you increase the movement time and decrease the waiting time quite considerably for each player. Simply by changing the game this much you begin to eliminate inappropriate social behavior that is exhibited by players who have to stand around and wait their turn. Although this concept is introduced now feel free to apply it to other types of games with a similar design. By mandating that it is a time limit game, you eliminate one team staying at bat for the whole play time. This concept also influences the kinds of social sanctions that result when a team stays in the field the whole time and can't ever seem to get up to bat.

MAGLADRY BALL

GAME 6-5. HIT AND GO (ELEMENTARY)

Players	Equipment	Movements	Organ. Pattern	Limitations	Purpose
same as game 6-3 but each batting team divides into 2 groups	same as game 6-3 except hula hoops represent bases	same as game 6-3	Random in field before ball is hit—after ball is hit, fielding team lines up in a file X X X X	1. Same as game 6-3 2. Same as game 6-3 3. Batter's job—hit the ball and run around 6 bases set in field like regular soft ball game—return home before the ball gets to out hoop. Batting team is divided into 2 groups—groups alternately bat—one member from each group bats and runs the bases, however the rest of the players in her batting group run the bases in a single file. 4. Fielder's job—one player fields the ball, rest of the fielders line up in a file with legs spread—the fielder with ball must crawl through her teammates' legs carrying the ball—she then runs the ball to the out hoop—if the ball reaches the out hoop before all of the batting group crosses home plate, an out is registered.	same as game 6-3

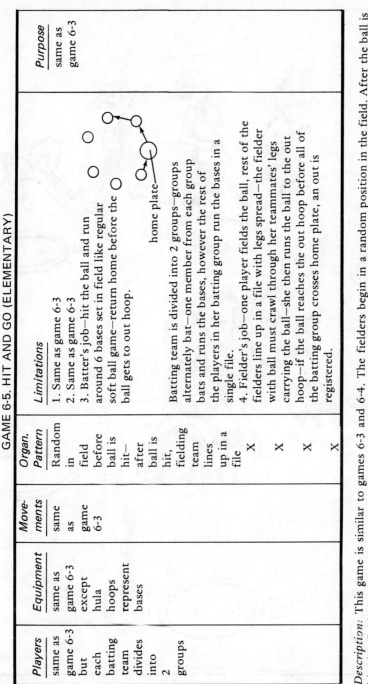

home plate

Description: This game is similar to games 6-3 and 6-4. The fielders begin in a random position in the field. After the ball is hit the fielding players line up one behind the other with their legs spread so the person retrieving the ball can finish the designed task. The batting team is divided equally into two groups, A and B. If A group is up (only one player hits), upon hitting the ball everyone in group A runs the bases in a single file. By splitting the batting team into two groups you now provide for some recovery time—this can become quite a strenuous game.

HIT AND GO

GAME 6-6. JUMP AND HIT (ELEMENTARY)

Players	Equipment	Movements	Organ. Pattern	Purpose
same as game 6-3	same as game 6-3 plus one jump rope	same as game 6-3 plus jumping rope		same as game 6-3 plus enhance jumping rope behavior

Limitations:

1. Same as game 6-3.
2. Same as game 6-3.
3. Batter's job: Upon hitting the ball, run to jump rope which is placed at opposite end of gym or field—jump rope 10 times—run back to home plate.
4. Fielder's job: Same as game 6-3.

Description: This game is essentially the same as game 6-3 but it introduces another motor skill not commonly found in softball—jumping rope. It is important to understand that you may have to change the numbers. The youngsters could either pass the ball or jump rope. Use the numbers appropriate for your youngsters. There is nothing sacred about those given in the game description.

GAME 6-7. COMBINATION SOFTBALL (ELEMENTARY)

Players	Equipment	Movements	Organ. Pattern	Purpose
any manageable number per team	hula hoops crash pads basketballs balls	running hitting forward rolls basketball shooting		promote development of the given motor skills plus begin to combine a variety of motor tasks

Limitations:

1. Similar to game 6-3 but increase batting time.
2. Same as game 6-3.
3. Batter must hit the ball and run to crash pads where he performs one, two, or three forward rolls—you choose—then he picks up basketball and stays until he scores 2 baskets, he then runs to home plate.
4. Same as game 6-3.

Description: The game is fairly self-descriptive. This game begins to combine a variety of movement tasks into a game. The game presupposes that each youngster has worked on the individual movement behaviors prior to their inclusion in a game form. This kind of game is excellent for getting the youngsters to think in alternatives relative to game design. This game also allows for individual interpretation of the tasks. For example, the task at the mats must be stated in the following manner: Perform any three forward type of rolls. Likewise the individual players are allowed to use any shooting style at the basketball area. Finally, this game has often been used to promote the design of many other games using skills not normally found in softball.

COMBINATION SOFTBALL

GAME 6-8. FIGURE 8 SOFTBALL (SECONDARY)

Players	Equipment	Movements	Organ. Pattern	Purpose
any manageable number per team	7 bases, 1 wooden stake, several types of bats, several types of balls	softball skills plus bowling in some cases	 X - pitcher O - home plate X - catcher	to develop motor skills—to account for each player's individual needs

Limitations:

1. Four outs per 1/2 inning.
2. How to make an out: basically the same as traditional softball—catch a fly, get the ball to the base before the runner, tag runner out.
3. Batter could choose type of bat and type of ball used each time he came to bat.
4. Throwing the bat was an automatic out.
5. Played 3 innings or until shower bell rang, whichever occurred first.
6. Stay at bat until you hit the ball forward.

Description: The game was played similarly to traditional softball. The batter had to run all 7 bases in proper order—first base to 7th base in a figure 8 pattern as illustrated in the organizational pattern category. The major difference was each batter chose the ball and bat and bat he used plus he dictated to the pitcher how he delivered the ball to the batter—rolled on the ground, thrown underhand, etc. The batter would then strike the ball and run to first base.

new kickball games. Thus you have 14 "new" games that you can now play at the elementary level. Many of the games described have been played at the secondary level by teachers in Montana, and the feedback received from these teachers has been quite positive. Game 6-8 was designed by some of the writer's high school students.

This proved to be a most interesting game. The students actually designed a game that began to account for individual hitting abilities. "Johnny Athlete" chose to hit a regular ball, while "Clumsie Charlie" chose to have the ball rolled toward him. The next thing to happen was that the students realized it was all right to exhibit their current motor ability. They began to see that they were different in motor ability, but each player could be accepted within the game structure on his current merits of ability.

This game led to a number of other games. One game they designed was similar to game 6-8, but each runner could run to any base at any time in any order. The only rule was that they had to touch each base before returning home. Sometimes three people would be on a base at one time. Soon even those kids who disliked physical education were asking to extend the class time—the biggest problem became getting the students to their next class on time.

VOLLEYBALL TYPE GAMES

The general movement behaviors found in volleyball type games must first be identified if the skills required in these games are to be developed. Volleyball games require that a player strike a moving ball, therefore all of the games must include this striking behavior. It is preposterous to claim that one is promoting volleyball behavior by requiring a youngster to catch a ball and then throw it back over the net. This is not to say that this is not a good skill to learn; rather it is simply not a volleyball type of skill. One can include the catch and throw motor behavior in a game but don't imagine that you will promote striking quickly. To develop the striking behavior you must require the students to strike at a ball. Yes, there are a multitude of factors that influence this skill, they must be accounted for in the game design. The following games are designed to promote volleyball skills, and it is hoped you can use them in your program.

GAME 6-9. KEEP IT GOING (ELEMENTARY)

Players	Equipment	Movements	Organ. Pattern	Limitations	Purpose
2 players per team	a ball of your choice	overhead striking underarm striking	pairs of players randomly scattered around gym	1. Must strike the ball in over head or underarm striking pattern. 2. You can hit it to yourself several times, then hit it to your partner. 3. You can play the ball off one bounce on the floor. 4. Try to keep the ball moving for 10 sec., 15 sec., 30 sec., teacher sets limit.	To enhance given motor skills. To promote coopera- tion among 2 players.

GAME 6-10. KEEP IT UP (ELEMENTARY)

Players	Equipment	Movements	Organ. Pattern	Limitations	Purpose
same as game 6-9				1. Same as game 6-9 2. Same as game 6-9 3. Must keep the ball off the floor, once it hits the floor, couple retrieves the ball and sits down. 4. Must keep the ball up for a period of time or for a certain number of hits between the two players; e.g., 6 hits, 12 hits.	same as game 6-9

Description: The game is self-explanatory. When first teaching the striking skill to these youngsters it is most important that they learn to control the ball. Therefore, the game is structured so the youngsters get the ball under control before they send it to their partner. The teacher controls the criteria determining when the game is over, i.e., certain number of hits or specific amount of time the ball must be kept off the floor.

GAME 6-11. KEEP IT UP OVER THE NET (ELEMENTARY)

Players	Equipment	Movements	Organ. Pattern	Limitations	Purpose
same as game 6-9	plus a net		couples facing each other with net between them	1. Same as game 6-9 2. Same as game 6-9 3. Same as game 6-10 plus you must strike it over the net to your partner so he can hit it back to you. 4. Same as game 6-10	To develop net skills with a ball. To promote cooperative behavior.

Description: The addition of a net is the only difference between this game and the previous two games. Make sure that you vary the height of the net and slope of the net.

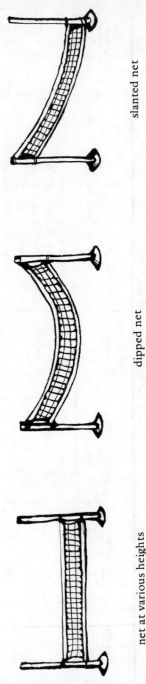

slanted net

dipped net

net at various heights

The height and slope variations allow the youngsters to pick the net type they can successfully cope with. There are dozens of versions of these three games—one can play each of the games with groups of 3, 4, 5, 6 players or more; likewise games 6-9 and 6-10 can be played with the players standing in a circle. You now have enough information to design several more games.

GAME 6-12. MASS VOLLEYBALL (ELEMENTARY)

Players	Equipment	Movements	Organ. Pattern	Limitations	Purpose
6-9/ team	ball of choice	volleyball striking skills	2 teams facing each other with net between the two of them.	1. Same as game 6-9 2. You can hit it several times to yourself then to a partner or hit the ball over the net to the other team. 3. If the ball hits the floor the opposing team gets a point regardless of who served the ball. 4. First team to score 10 points is the winner. 5. You cannot hit the net with your body - forfeit point if you do.	To develop team play using volleyball skills. To develop cooperative behavior.

Description: This game is played like regular volleyball except for the rule changes. There is no service area, so the person closest to the ball can serve it from their position. There are no prescribed positions, thus everyone is involved in the game.

GAME 6-13. THREE HITS (ELEMENTARY)

Players	Equipment	Movements	Organ. Pattern	Limitations	Purpose
same as game 6-12				1. Same as game 6-9 2. A team can only hit the ball 3 times on one side and the ball must go over the net on the third hit—one player can hit it 3 times. 3. Same as game 6-12 4. Same as game 6-12 5. Same as game 6-12	Same as game 6-12.

Description: This game is similar to game 6-12 except now you are mandating that the players control the ball even more because the 3 hit limit suggests better control.

One can add an additional ball or two into games 6-12 and 6-13 if increased movement time per individual player is desired. Likewise you can use a variety of ball types in these games. Elementary youngsters usually prefer the plastic balls or the inside of a basketball—the bladder. Do not hesitate to apply previously learned games analysis concepts when altering these games.

GAME 6-14. FOUR CORNERS VOLLEYBALL (ELEMENTARY)

Players	Equipment	Movements	Organ. Pattern	Purpose
3-6 players per team; 4 teams per net arrangement	4-6 balls per game	same as game 6-12	(diagram) 2 nets crisscrossed with a team in each quadrant	To develop visual tracking behavior. To develop alertness in youngsters during game.

```
        X           X  X
    X   X       X   X

    X   X           X
        X  X
```

2 nets crisscrossed with a team in each quadrant

Limitations:

All the rules are similar to games 6-12 and 6-13 except that initially no points are kept. Each team begins with one or two balls. The object is to play against the other three quadrants. See game description below.

Description: The players must be alert at all times. The object of the game is to have no balls in your quadrant. It is each team for themselves. Upon the go signal from the teacher, each team, using volleyball skills attempts to get the balls to the other teams. The game looks almost like a free-for-all but the youngsters enjoy it very much. The teacher stops the game when one team seems to have the majority of the balls.

GAME 6-14 FOUR CORNERS VOLLEYBALL

SECONDARY

The games described in this section lead towards regulation volleyball. Many of the elementary games can be adapted to the secondary level as you will soon see.

GAME 6-15. FOUR HITS (SECONDARY)

Players	Equipment	Movements	Organ. Pattern	Limitations	Purpose
5-8/ team 2 teams per game	1 ball/ game you chose the ball	overhead and underarm striking skills	two teams facing each other with a net between the two of them.	1. Each player may hit the ball only once. 2. Each team may only hit the ball 4 times on one side and the ball must go over on the 4th hit. 3. If the ball hits the floor, the opposing team gets a point. 4. Ball must be served behind the service line (15'-20' from net) 5. Can only score when you are serving the ball. 6. If the non-serving team makes the ball hit the floor on the opposing team's side, the non-serving team "wins" the serve. 7. Game is 15 points.	To develop the given motor skills. To introduce volleyball rules. To promote co-operative team behavior.

Description: The game is played much like regulation volleyball. The major difference is that each team is allowed four hits on a side before sending the ball over to the other team. The purpose is quite simple. Allow the players to control the ball before hitting it.

GAME 6-16 is called THREE HITS—each team is allowed only 3 hits and then the ball must go over. Vary the type of ball used and height of the net when designing volleyball games for this age student.

GAME 6-17. SET AND SPIKE (SECONDARY)

Players	Equipment	Movements	Organ. Pattern	Limitations	Purpose
same as game 6-15		plus spike	↑	1. Same as game 6-16 2. The ball may only be hit three times on one side; third hit needs to be a spike. 3. Same as game 6-15 4. Same as game 6-15 5. Same as game 6-15 6. Same as game 6-15 7. Same as game 6-15	Same as game 6-15 plus teaching how to spike a ball.

Description: The only rule change is that the ball must be hit 3 times on a side with the third hit being a spike. The game looks like a traditional volleyball game.

GAME 6-18 simply introduces the circle rotation of the players upon receiving the serve. Otherwise the game is similar to traditional. Secondary students like to design other versions of this game using a variety of balls and other pieces of equipment.

BASKETBALL TYPE GAMES

This game area is perhaps the easiest one in which students can begin to modify the game structure. Experience at both the elementary and secondary level has shown that the students are capable of adapting equipment, altering rules, and even changing or adding additional movement patterns, and are willing or even eager to do so. All of the games described below have been played and enjoyed by the students. Some of them reflect the traditional form of basketball while others may not appear to you like a basketball game at all.

GAME 6-19. ONE X ONE (ELEMENTARY)

Players	Equipment	Movements	Organ. Pattern	Limitations	Purpose
2/ game	1 ball—you decide what kind	all basketball movements	random 1/2 court	1. NO traveling, double dribble 2. Call own fouls, foul results in ball taken in from sidelines. 3. 3/pts./basket 4. 15 pts wins game 5. winner of basket maintains possession 6. 1 pt./hula hoop score	To develop shooting, dribbling, offensive and defensive skills.
	1 hula hoop				

Description: Game begins with one player inbounding ball. Offensive player may shoot at basket or at hula hoop hung from basket. Winner of basket maintains possession of ball. Play is similar to traditional basketball.

GAME 6-20. PASS AND SHOOT (ELEMENTARY)

Players	Equipment	Movements	Organ. Pattern	Limitations	Purpose
couples, unlimited	1 ball/ couple	pass shoot	couples random in gym	1. Teacher indicated number of passes and shots to be taken per couple. 2. Must perform passes first, then one person performs prescribed number of shots, return to partner, sit down.	To develop pass and shooting skills.

Description: Couples face each other, 5' apart. Teacher writes large P & S on board with number under P & S. Players must then pass ball number indicated. One player shoots 'til basket is made. Return to partner, sit quietly.

This game promotes a great deal of movement time for passing and shooting. If you asked your students to practice passing the ball back and forth 50 times they would get very bored. However, putting the same movement task in a game form, I have found that the youngsters can perform 100-200 passes per session and still enjoy the game. The youngsters have altered the movement from the passing spot to the shooting area. For example, they suggested that you carry the ball, hop with the ball, run backwards with the ball, move in pairs passing the ball back and forth and many other movement tasks. They have also given the player who remains at the passing site a task to perform such as moving the ball in a figure 8 pattern around the legs. Can you share some ideas with us?

GAME 6-21. FOUR CORNER RELAY (ELEMENTARY)

Players	Equipment	Movements	Organ. Pattern	Purpose
5-8/ team	1 ball/ team	dribbling passing		To develop dribbling skill.

Limitations:

1. Each team has first player dribble ball to gym center.
2. Must dribble ball with one hand.
3. May not bump into anybody or you must begin again.
4. First team to return to original starting position wins.
5. Must be sitting down.

Description: First person from each team dribbles to center of gym, all four crisscross one with the other. Each player continues diagonally to opposite corner of gym, hands ball off to next player who in turn dribbles to gym center. Original dribbler gets at end of line he has dribbled to. Play continues until all players return to starting position.

With this game you first have to ask your youngsters to run the pattern without the ball. The youngsters may be able to add a second ball for each team as they become more proficient.

Within the framework of this game, the youngsters have combined movement tasks or changed the movement directional order. Feel free to alter the game and come up with many more versions.

GAME 6-22. PASS AND TURN (ELEMENTARY)

Players	Equipment	Movements	Organ. Pattern	Purpose
4-8/ team	1 ball/ team	pass and dribble	X X X X X X X X X Columns facing other end of gym	To develop pass and dribble skills.

Limitations:

1. Each player may only dribble with one hand, must chest pass.
2. Each player must stop at designated spot on floor.
3. First team to have all players pass and turn wins.
4. Must be sitting on floor to end game.

Description: First player from each team dribbles ball to opposite end of gym, returns while dribbling ball to spot indicated on floor, performs chest pass to teammate who also dribbles to opposite end of gym, returns to mark on floor (5' from other player.) He passes ball to first player who turns and passes to next person in line. This person and every other person in line must weave in and out of players standing on gym floor to other end of gym, return to spot on gym floor, pass to next player who passes to next and so on down the line until ball reaches starting column. Play continues until each player has dribbled ball and passed ball and is standing in line on gym floor.

GAME 6-22 PASS AND TURN

GAME 6-23. PASS, TURN AND SHOOT (ELEMENTARY)

Players	Equipment	Movements	Organ. Pattern	Purpose
same as game 6-22		plus shooting		Same as game 6-22 plus improving shooting skills.

Limitations:

1. Same as preceding game but add following rules: Each player one at a time, gets to shoot at either basket (3 pts.) or at the hula hoop (1 pt.) hung from basket.
2. After shooting return via a dribble to next player in line.
3. Game is over when each player has shot once.
4. Most points win the game.
5. The shooting occurs after the pass and turn relay has been performed.

Description: Players perform pass and turn relay first. Then while standing in line one at a time the players try to score a basket via hula hoop or regular basket. Game is over when each person has taken one shot.

GAME 6-23 PASS, TURN AND SHOOT

GAME 6-24 BASKETBOWL

GAME 6-24. BASKETBOWL (ELEMENTARY)

Players	Equipment	Movements	Organ. Pattern	Purpose
any number per team do not have to have even numbers per team—the more teams you have, the greater is the movement time	variety of balls hula hoops bowling pins or something like them	all basketball movements plus bowling movements	relay formation--you decide--could be: X X X X X X X X X X X X X X X	To develop strategy to promote motor skill development.

Limitations:

1. Time limit game—3 minutes.
2. Scoring system—1 point/pin knocked over, 2 points for putting ball through hula hoop, 3 points for putting ball through basket.
3. May only have one chance at bowling and may only take one shot at basket.
4. Must hand the ball to next player on your team.

Description: The teams are in any relay pattern you desire. The first player on each team attempts to bowl the ball and knock over a pin or pins set up 20'-30' away—preferably in front of wall. Having completed this task, the player retrieves the ball and moves (you decide) to the shooting area where he takes one shot at either the basket or the hula hoop hanging from the basket. He then gets the rebound and moves (you decide) back to his team and hands the ball to the next player.

This is a fantastic game because it accounts for the youngsters who can't shoot; they can still score points for the team by bowling. By adding a second ball into the game you can improve the movement time and decrease the waiting time. By

BASKETBOWL (continued)

changing a component or categories you can design dozens of more games using the basic framework. I allow the teams to develop strategies for getting the ball quickly to each teammate. This game can be played in a relatively small gym. To provide for less confusion at the shooting area, it is suggested that you set the gym up in the following manner:

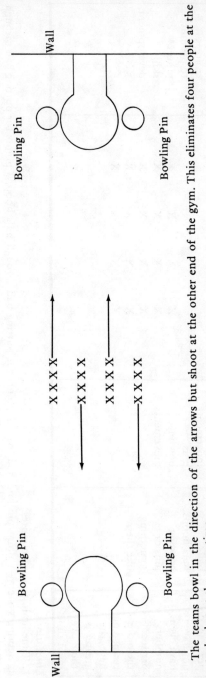

The teams bowl in the direction of the arrows but shoot at the other end of the gym. This eliminates four people at the same basket at the same time.

GAME 6-25. BOUNCE BALL (SECONDARY)

Players	Equipment	Movements	Organ. Pattern	Limitations	Purpose
7/team	1 large ball 1 small ball	running, passing, hopping	random	1. Must one hand dribble ball in selected areas. 2. Must hop while dribbling ball in marked area. 3. One point for ball through basket in traditional manner; 3 points if you can bounce ball into basket. Double points using small ball. 4. Game over when 15 points are scored. 5. Play both balls independently of one another.	To develop shooting and passing skills.

Description: There are 7 players on the court from each team at the same time. The game is conducted much like traditional basketball but with more players and different types of balls, additional rules and additional hopping movement.

GAME 6-26. HOCKEY BALL (SECONDARY)

Players	Equipment	Movements	Organ. Pattern	Limitations	Purpose
5-8/ team	2 balls, 2 bats, 4 lummey sticks	running, dribbling, shooting	random	1. Play both balls independently of one another. 2. The lummey sticks are used to dribble the balls in specifically marked areas by hitting the balls with the sticks. 3. Each team has one bat and is allowed to stand under its own basket and by sticking the bat up through the net, may try to prevent a ball from going through. 4. Bat may only be held vertically by one player in specially marked area beneath defensive basket. 5. Four points for each basket; time limit game, you decide.	to develop shooting, passing strategy skills

Description: Each team gets 1 ball, 1 bat and 2 lummey sticks. The game is much like traditional basketball except in designated areas the ball must be dribbled via lummey sticks. Balls may be blocked by a goalie with a bat positioned up through the net. All other traditional basketball skills may be employed.

GAME 6-26 HOCKEY BALL

GAME 6-27. BACK-BACK BASKETBALL (SECONDARY)

Players	Equipment	Movements	Organ. Pattern	Limitations	Purpose
any # up to 7/team	2 balls/ game	all regular basketball movements	random	1. Use 2 basketball courts which are back-to-back, see diagram. 2. Each team gets one ball, both balls are put into play at same time. 3. Must shoot at basket not facing your team at beginning of game. 4. To begin game each team lines up facing basket they will defend (see diagram). 5. Regular basketball rules are then followed. After a score you must take ball out-of-bounds at mid-court of your own defensive basket.	to develop basketball skills to promote problem-solving

Description: The only differences between this game and the traditional game is that 2 balls are used and you use 2 baskets that are back to back. All basketball skills are used. After a basket has been made, the ball must be returned to original start position before being thrown in again. Usually plastic cones or mid-court lines designate this boundary.

The back to back basketball game became a favorite among several of my high school senior classes. They adjusted the rules as they needed to. Most important, they decided upon the rule changes prior to beginning play.

With each of the previously described games, the door is open for change. Often times the students will ask you for certain types of equipment, things that may appear to be "junk." Our school did not have a large physical education equipment budget, as a matter of fact we usually received the athletic rejects (equipment). Thus we made every effort to find a use for each and every item we had. Instead of discarding broken bats, the students found an effective use for them. Many students started to bring their "junk" equipment to school. It became quite a challenge to the students to figure out (solve a problem) how to incorporate the "equipment" into a game. The students would use various types of balls not traditionally meant to be used in the sport of basketball. They used everything from small plastic balls to basketball bladders extracted from worn out basketballs. Many times the students would use regulation basketballs in combination with other types of balls.

Can you think of some other ways to alter the traditional game? You can see that most of the changes made by the students occurred in the Equipment, Movement and Organizational Pattern categories. By trial and error and by logical thinking the students developed a multitude of games that they found enjoyable to play. Many of the students began to think about game strategy and category relationship for the first time.

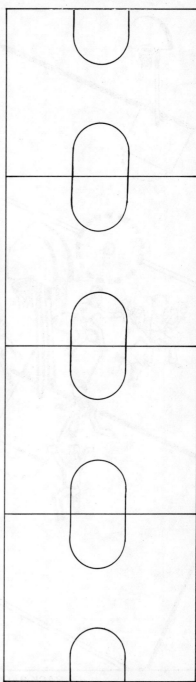

BACK-BACK BASKETBALL COURTS

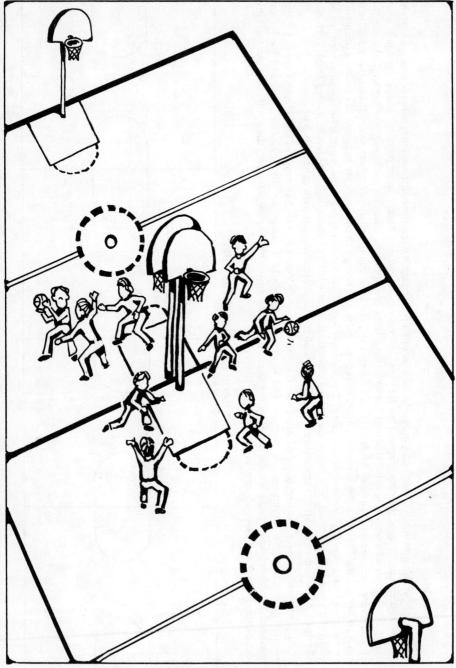

BACK-BACK BASKETBALL

TAG AND RELAY GAMES

Each· tag and relay game should be played for a purpose. For example, tag games should be played to help develop motor control while relay games should be played to enhance specific motor skills and to begin combining motor skills. Before playing a tag game a great deal of noncompetitive motor control work should be performed. The youngsters should be able to control all of their body parts while moving; they should exhibit excellent dodging behavior and stopping ability. All of these movement prerequisites should be met before the youngsters are allowed to play a tag game. In addition they should be taught how to tag gently. The following is an example of a method for promoting such behaviors.

Using a tamborine, shaking the tamborine means to move, hitting the tamborine means to stop. I ask the youngsters to run in a variety of directions without touching anyone. I call this the "Don't Touch Me" game. Over time I gradually decrease the boundaries within which they are allowed to move until they are moving in a small area without touching one another. Do not sit the youngster out who may be running into people, but also don't let this behavior continue. This is the way I address this kind of behavior.

First I recue the group—"Nineteen people are running without touching one another." I focus the attention on the desired task, not the undesired task. Early in my teaching career I would have said, "Great—only two people are bumping into one another." You know what happens. This gives the idea to four or five kids that bumping onto one another sounds like a neat idea. If the youngster is still bumping into other youngsters I proceed to step #2—ask her what the task is. "Mary, what are you supposed to be doing?" Mary will say, "Running without touching anyone." You say, "Mary, show me that you can do that." If Mary still continues to bump you now move to step #3. "Mary, you have a decision to make; continue bumping and you get to sit with me; show me no bumping and you stay in the game. You decide, I'll give you five seconds for a decision." Wait five seconds and ask the youngster; she usually performs well. If she doesn't, then follow through on the time-out of the game action. You now say to Mary, "I see, Mary, that *you* have decided to sit out." The major behavioral concept that the teacher is employing is that the youngster accepts responsibility for her own behavior. I firmly believe that we need a course at educational institutions on how to talk to youngsters. There are many everyday behavioral situations that must be met and handled properly—often what one says or how it is said promotes the resultant child behavior.

TAG

The following tag games are not necessarily unique. Many are traditional, some are creative—please use them sparingly in a movement program and use them only after leading the youngsters into them properly. The format is changed for this section. The games will merely be described for you, since by now you understand how to use the grid to alter any game.

COUPLES TAG

Start with two or three youngsters as "it." The object of the game is to be the last one caught. There is no home base or any way not to be caught. Everyone starts moving—as soon as one "it" tags another player they join hands and now both of them are "it." The couple tries to tag another player who joins hands with them—there are now three people in the group. Once the group of three tags another player (group of four), the group splits in half or into couples. This process continues until all the youngsters are caught—usually ending with a number of couples.

HIP TUNNEL TAG

Start with two or three youngsters "it." The object of the game is never to get tagged. If you are tagged, you freeze in a standing position with legs spread shoulder width and hands on hips. To get unfrozen someone must go between your legs—once this is done you are free to continue moving.

ADD-ON TAG

This is similar to couples tag except you never let go of hands or break into smaller groups. As you are tagged you "add-on" to those already tagged by joining their hands. The object is to be the last one caught. After a few minutes there is usually a long line. Don't allow the youngsters to kick at a player as they try to go under the line.

BACK-TO-BACK TAG

This is exactly like hip tunnel tag except that you cannot be tagged if you are standing back to back with a friend.

OCTOPUS TAG

The floor is marked off as follows:

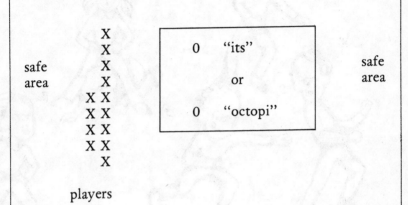

The players try to make it across to the other safe area. If tagged, they become the octopus' helping arm. They must keep one foot frozen to the floor, they can pivot on it, and as players run by they can tag them. Once tagged, you become the octopi helpers. The two octopi are free to move around in the gym except in the safe areas. You cannot be tagged in the safe areas. This tag game is a favorite among the 5th and 6th graders.

RELAYS

Relays are fun but again should be played with a purpose in mind. The following format will be adopted:

1. Identify the various organizational patterns.
2. Suggest the kind of behaviors resulting from each organizational pattern.
3. Describe specific relays.

HIP TUNNEL TAG

1. IDENTIFICATION OF THE
VARIOUS RELAY PATTERNS

There is a wide variety of organizational relay patterns. Some are described below, but of course there are many others.

A.

X X X X X X X X X X

X X X X X X X X X X

file formation

B.

X X X   X X X

X X X   X X X

shuttle formation

C.

```
      X  X  X
   X          X
   X          X
   X          X
      X  X  X
```

circle

D.

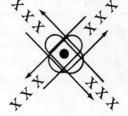

four corners formation

E.

X X X X X X

X

line or column formation

F.

X   X   X

X   X

X

triangle formation

These are the basic formations—you can have double circle, double file, etc. formations. Each is unique in the kind of behavior that results because of its design.

2. RESULTANT BEHAVIOR DUE TO
RELAY PATTERN DESIGN

The file formation enhances waiting in line, inappropriate social behavior, and emotional outbursts. Dependent upon the number of youngsters on a team, the waiting time/movement time ratio favors the waiting time. Youngsters usually get one turn and then stand in line. This standing in line with nothing to do often leads to bumping and hitting behavior. This inappropriate social behavior is the direct result of the pattern design. In addition, inappropriate emotional outbursts by teams often result if they lose the relay—if the teams are lined up side by side, the mere proximity to the other teams and the standing in line behavior causes the youngsters' attention to focus on the other team. If the team loses, it is immediately visible to all. A suggestion to eliminate this behavior is to use either a circle or four corners relay formation.

The shuttle relay formation automatically improves the movement time and decreases the waiting time—the youngsters are given more turns—but the same kinds of social and emotional problems can arise with this pattern unless the teams are spread out on the floor. If proximity of teams is a leading factor in the youngsters exhibiting inappropriate behavior, simply move the teams. There is nothing sacred about having the teams side by side.

EXAMPLE:

Team 1		*Team 2*	*Team 3*
X X X	X X X	X	X
		X	X
		X	X
		X	X
		X	X
		X	X

Team 4

X
  X
    X

      X
       X
        X

The distance between the two groups within each team stays constant, the change is in team position on the floor. Try shifting the team position and see what happens.

By design the circle formation allows the team members to focus attention on their performance. Many of the youngsters have their backs turned to the other teams and thus cannot see what the others are doing.

The four corners formation can be used in a variety of ways. Each corner group can represent an individual team, or, groups diagonally facing one another can represent one team.

The line and triangle formations simply improve movement time and decrease waiting time.

Before describing a few relays here is another thought. Usually the level of the group, i.e., the height of the group from the floor, is the same—standing level. Experiments with various team levels, kneeling, sitting, lying on floor have shown that the youngsters love them; moreover, a variety of behavioral outcomes result. In addition, there is nothing sacred about one person per relay moving at a time. Why not have two, three, or four members of a relay team moving at the same time?

Below are descriptions of some creative relays that my elementary youngsters designed.

RELAYS

1. MATH CIRCLE RELAY—All teams are in a circle formation lying on their stomachs with their heads facing the center of the circle. Each team numbers off from 1 to as many members as they have on the team. The teacher gives the teams a math problem such as: 2 + 2 =   . Whoever has the number of the correct answer stands up and runs around the team, stepping over each team member. Upon arriving back to his starting position, he resumes his prone position. The teacher immediately gives another problem. You can have two, three, or four members of the same team running at the same time. The teacher controls the tempo of the game. Variations include other math operations and other movement tasks.

2. OPPOSITION ADD-ON—The teams are in a four corners relay pattern.

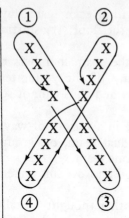

Team 3 does the same thing as Team 1

Team 4 does the same thing as Team 2

A member of Team 1 runs to the opposite team, going all the way around it, returns to her team, goes around it, joins hands with her second team member. This process is repeated until all the team members have joined hands and run the distance. The relay is over once this task is completed. All four teams do the same task.

3. *SHUTTLE TASKS*–All three teams are in a shuttle relay formation, i.e., each team is divided in half with both halves facing one another.

	①				④		
wall	X X X a		center of gym		d X X X		
	②				⑤		
	X X X b				e X X X		wall
	③				⑥		
	X X X c				f X X X		

All the team members are facing the center of the gym. The first member of each group, designated a b c d e f must perform the following tasks in any order: touch the wall behind them, touch the wall across from them, and go through the legs of the opposing group. Having finished those tasks he returns to his own group and tags the next player.

This relay dramatically increases movement time and even creates a task for those who are waiting their turn.

4. *DRIBBLE-JUMP-ROLL-RELAY*—All teams are in a four corners pattern.

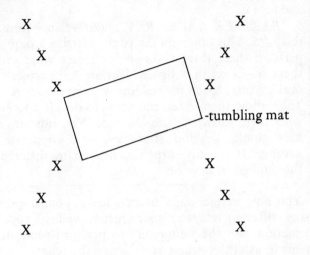

Each team must perform the following tasks: jump rope three times, dribble a ball to the mat, perform a forward rolling movement, dribble the ball back to team, and hand the ball to the next team member. On each team, the member at the end of the team must shoot 2 baskets, score 2 points for each basket, return to team. Relay is over when everyone has performed all tasks once. Thus there could be two ways to win: first team finished or team that scores the most points. Thus another concept has been introduced—allow the waiting participants an opportunity to perform while waiting, yet build in some rest time.

5. *PARTNER RACES*—These can be performed in twos or threes. Partners line up and face each other 15'-20' apart.

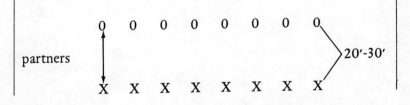

On command by the teacher, the circles run up to partners (X's) crawl through their legs, run around partner, proceed to nearest black line and touch it with their noses, return to starting position and sit down. Immediately switch positions and repeat.

6. *PARTNER RACES REVISITED*—Same formation as in relay #5. This time you say to the starting group: "You must perform these three tasks—I don't care what order you do them in—crawl in a figure eight around partner's legs, jump over partner, touch the red line with an elbow, return home." Then allow them a few moments to decide upon the strategy with their partners. Run the race. You now are making the kids think, develop strategies, and cooperate with one another. It is really surprising how many different strategies the youngsters develop.

You now have enough information at your disposal to design as many different relays as your creativity allows you. Simply take a formation, ask the youngsters to perform some different movements or ask the youngsters to design the relay.

The model on the next page may help you design the relays.

All you have to do is pick an item or more from each category and you have a new relay. Notice that your suggestions really are more important than the ones presented in this section.

The examples provided in this chapter can be incorporated into your program, but it is also hoped that they have stimulated some new thoughts relative to providing movement examples in each of the listed areas.

References

Kirchner, Glenn. *Physical Education for Elementary School Children.* Dubuque, Iowa: William C. Brown Co., 1974.

Cratty, Bryant. *Active Learning.* Englewood Cliffs, N.J.: Prentice-Hall, 1971.

RELAY FORMATION

Relay Formations	Movements	Rules	Team Positions
circle	run	time limit relay	side by side
file	jump	each person does each task once	opposite one another
four corners	skip rope		close to each other
shuttle	dribble a ball	each person does each task twice	far away from each other
triangle	forward rolls		scattered
line	run backwards	first team finished	???
double circle	cartwheels	team scores most pts.	
double line	3-legged run ???	???	
???			

Chapter

Some
Closing Thoughts

All teachers bring to their classes a set of beliefs and a set of biases regarding *what* should be taught and *how* it should be taught. Each one of us wants to repeat our successes and eliminate our failures as we teach day to day. Certainly at the elementary school level an important part of the physical education curriculum is an area known as games. All of us have our own opinion as to their worth in the total development of our students. Some of us teach games for recreation purposes while others of us teach games for specific motoric reasons. Regardless of what we think games can do for youngsters, it is absolutely imperative that we understand that games must be designed in specific ways in order for certain behaviors to result. Hoping that a youngster will become a "better sport" and/or saying that a game enhances emotional self-confidence is like trying to drive from Los Angeles to Death Valley in mid-July without any water in the car. You find out partway through your journey that you forgot a most important item—water. It is the same way with games; if the teacher has not carefully structured the game, partway through the game it turns out that an item is missing—the design of the game is mandating the behavioral outcome. I believe that teachers must reevaluate the role of games in an elementary physical education class in light of the objectives stated for the class and that teachers need to understand the relationships between game designs and behavioral outcomes if they want *each* youngster to develop to his or her capacity within a game environment. This statement presupposes that all teachers realize that youngsters develop physically, emotionally, socially, and intellectually at various rates but in similar patterns. It also presupposes that all teachers are aware of the stages of development. This book has attempted to describe briefly the developmental stages through which youngsters seem to progress, and, through the medium of games, to share with you some ideas on how to structure games in order to account for individual differences. It is hoped that as a result you will question the role, use, and value of certain game designs. You see, it is not necessarily essential that elementary youngsters learn *the way* to hand dribble a regulation basketball or perform an instep kick in soccer. An elementary program's sole responsibility is not necessarily to prepare youngsters for junior and senior high movement physical education game and sport programs. Rather, sequencing motor patterns or movement behaviors for individual youngsters should be considered just as important as learning specific sports skills.

Vern Seefeldt (1972) at Michigan State University has spent years developing a curriculum for elementary youngsters that attempts to sequence movements for youngsters. It is important to have a tool to exhibit this idea. Hopefully, games analysis begins to allow teachers to skillfully sequence movement activities within the games movement environment.

It is also important to deal with the whole child rather than attempt to segregate a youngster's life into separate entities. Thus it is our role to concern ourselves with the emotional, social, and intellectual development of our youngsters. No longer can we say that it is someone else's job to teach youngsters how to cooperate, how to express inner feelings, how to compete, how to employ human relation strategies—it is *all* teachers roles to do this. When someone says to me that education should be a reflection of the real world, I first ask why, and secondly I ask him to state in specific observable behaviors what he means. You see, I am not sure that many of us can find the handle on identifying specific behaviors. Games analysis in its very limited fashion is an attempt to provide the teacher with a tool that helps identify behaviors and teach to those same behaviors.

Finally, youngsters must be involved in rational decision-making processes. Making decisions and realizing that there are consequences to the decisions made is a learned behavior. Because decision making involves a process, this suggests that teachers have a tool they can use to develop each youngster's decision making ability. Games analysis, limited as it is, attempts to provide the teacher with a tool to use in developing this ability.

Games are important to youngsters and adults. Let us critically analyze their use in physical education programs. Let us realize that games, in and of themselves should not be *the* curriculum for our programs, rather games represent only one of the mediums through which youngsters learn about themselves. Perhaps we need to investigate the entire structure of our curriculum in light of "Are we really consistent in our curriculum design and the outcomes expected from its design?" Perhaps our educational beliefs are not really properly reflected in the types of movement experiences we provide for our students. This is why I think that it is most important to understand what games can do for and do against youngsters. Yes, it is time to know How to Change the Games Children Play.

References

Seefeldt, Vern. "Sequencing Motor Skills within the Physical Education Curriculum." Paper presented at AAHPER National Convention, Houston, Texas, March 27, 1972.

Mosston, Muska. *Teaching Physical Education.* Columbus, Ohio: Charles E. Merrill Publishing Co., 1966.

Appendix—

Factors and Choices *

CATCHING

	Color of Ball	Background Color	Speed of Flight
Easy	blue	white	10 m.p.h.
↓	yellow	black	15 m.p.h.
	orange	black	20 m.p.h.
	red	white	25 m.p.h.
	green	yellow	30 m.p.h.
Difficult	??	??	??

	Angle of Trajectory	Texture of Ball	
Easy	Horizontal		balloon
↓	Vertical	soft<	beach ball
	Arc		nerf ball
	???		
			playground ball
		firm<	bladder of balls
			rubber balls
			softballs
		hard<	whiffle balls
			baseballs
Difficult			??

*The factors shown here are by no means all that influence these movement behaviors. They represent examples, and readers are invited to share their ideas with us.

KICKING

	Position of Ball Movement	Type of Kick
Easy	stationary	toe kick
↓	horizontally rolling	instep kick
	bouncing roll	punt
	ball in flight	outside foot kick
Difficult	??	??

	Texture of Ball	Shape of Object	Anticipation Location
Easy	beachball	cardboard box	no step and kick
↓	playground ball	milk carton	take a step - kick
	all purpose ball	round ball	take 3 steps - kick
	soccer ball	oblong ball	run distance - kick
	football	??	??
Difficult	??		

JUMPING

	Type of Jump	Landing Surface	Body Position
Easy	jump down	crash pads	compact
↓	horizontal jump	saw dust pit	
	vertical jump	gym mat	extended
	??	concrete surface	??
Difficult		??	

BODY ROLLING

	Body Position	Body Speed while Rolling	Direction of Roll
Easy	compact	slow	forward
↓	tucked		sideways
↓	curled	↓	backwards
↓	piked		??
↓	extended	fast	
Difficult	??	??	

	Initiation Height of Roll	Distance From Start Point to Roll Initiation
Easy	close to mat-squat	1 ft.
↓	bent over position	2 ft.
↓	standing position	3 ft.
↓	jump to roll	5 ft.
Difficult	??	??